Blue Portugal and Other Essays

Theresa Kishkan

Blue Portugal

& Other Essays

UNIVERSITY *of* **ALBERTA** PRESS

Published by

University of Alberta Press
1–16 Rutherford Library South
11204 89 Avenue NW
Edmonton, Alberta, Canada T6G 2J4
Amiskwacîwâskahican | Treaty 6 |
Métis Territory
uap.ualberta.ca | uapress@ualberta.ca

LIBRARY AND ARCHIVES CANADA
CATALOGUING IN PUBLICATION

Title: Blue Portugal and other essays /
    Theresa Kishkan.
Names: Kishkan, Theresa, author.
Series: Wayfarer (Edmonton, Alta.)
Description: Series statement: Wayfarer |
    Includes bibliographical references.
Identifiers: Canadiana (print) 2022015998X |
    Canadiana (ebook) 20220159998 |
    ISBN 9781772125993 (softcover) |
    ISBN 9781772126167 (EPUB) |
    ISBN 9781772126174 (PDF)
Subjects: LCGFT: Essays.
Classification: LCC PS8571.I75 B58 2022 |
    DDC C814/.54—dc23

First edition, first printing, 2022.
First printed and bound in Canada by
Houghton Boston Printers, Saskatoon,
Saskatchewan.
Copyediting by Kimmy Beach.
Proofreading by Mary Lou Roy.

Every effort has been made to identify
copyright holders and obtain permission for
the use of copyright material. Please notify
University of Alberta Press of any additions
or corrections that should be incorporated in
future reprints or editions of this book.

University of Alberta Press is committed to
protecting our natural environment. As part
of our efforts, this book is printed on Enviro
Paper: it contains 100% post-consumer recycled fibres and is acid- and chlorine-free.

University of Alberta Press gratefully
acknowledges the support received for its
publishing program from the Government
of Canada, the Canada Council for the Arts,
and the Government of Alberta through the
Alberta Media Fund.

for my family

Who knows if in that darkness he might still
have spoken, and I answered?
*   But my heart*
longed, after this, to see the dead elsewhere.

—*ODYSSEY*, Book 11, lines 564–567, trans. Robert Fitzgerald

Contents

Preface

I BEGAN MY WRITING LIFE AS A POET, publishing two poetry collections in my twenties. I stopped writing for nearly a decade after the births of three children. My husband and I were building a house for our family on 8.5 acres of wooded land on a peninsula northwest of Vancouver. I created a garden and learned the art of quilt-making. I expected to have time to write again once my children were in school and I expected to return to poetry, but I was surprised to discover that poetry no longer wanted me. I had the impulse to write, I had ideas to explore, materials accumulating in my mind as my quilting basket accumulated scraps of cotton, but I didn't have a shape for my thinking any longer. The lines I wrote continued past the point where a poet would consider the stanza, the lyric, complete. At first I tried to wrangle them, contain them, but one day I just let those lines continue, as prose, maintaining a certain rhythm but given the freedom of the wide space on a page. One line led to another, then another. Their purpose was not to create fiction but instead to make a map of my own reflections, main roads and secondary roads, river systems, mountains, and beautiful circled stars for settlements. One line led to another, a thread leading me into the heart of meaning I hoped would be there, a little knot at the centre. I remember how exhilarated I felt to discover I was writing something that I came to understand was an essay.

In an interview[1] about the anthology *The Making of the American Essay*, John D'Agata talks about his quest to look at essays in a different light, to consider them as capturing the activity of human thought in real time. In many ways this is a logical progression of Michel de Montaigne's sixteenth-century essays, the noun essai meaning a trial or an attempt, yoked to the verb essayer (Old French), to try, from the late Latin *exagium*, meaning a balance or a weight. Many of us grew up learning the essay as a formal container for critical analysis but the form has evolved—or we have, in our relationship to the form—in the way a plant might evolve, hybridize in response to new soil conditions, weather, and use requirements. It's the later possibilities of the essay that interest me most—its generous capacity to hold a writer's interests in subject matter, as well as moments of poetry, phrases of song, recipes for really good soup, analysis of data, interrogation of known facts, how these can be braided in a simple three-strand arrangement of ideas or themes or a more elaborate imbricated confection that allows stray tendrils, and how the writing can use the entire page as a kind of open map, a musical score, or a grammar of pattern language. It's not that I want to abandon traditional narrative as a mode of expression. In some of the essays in *Blue Portugal*, narrative is employed to shape a story that interests me, a family story for which I am aware of only fragments of the whole; by attending to the possibilities of the story, how it might be brought to light if I ask questions of it, survey the historical record, and arrange the story's elements this way and that, superimposing a literal archival map on the liminal spaces of memory, I am often rewarded with a version of the truth. It's that idea of John D'Agata's again: the activity of human thought in real time.

Some essay collections are unified thematically or chronologically around a writer's life so that a reader understands the book to be a form of memoir. *Blue Portugal* does not aspire to memoir, exactly. There are connections between the individual essays, yes, there are times when they talk among themselves, refer the reader to others in the group, but my intention was not to create a unified set of texts, with a logical flow. What the essays share is a sensibility—mine, of course, but also I know that I am interested in ideas and terrain which often share something in common. The rivers of my home province echo the venous system of my body. The indigo powder I turn into dye in turn shares a palette with entoptic phenomena. The title essay remembers a wine I first drank in my grandmother's homeland. These are personal essays after all, not rhetorical or expository ones, so I'm at the heart of each one. Mine is the voice that invites the reader in, welcomes you at the door. My heart is on the sleeve of each essay. I'm the woman on the raft in the Thompson River and in the restaurant in Prague, in the PET tunnel in the BC Cancer Agency, portioning out her parents' ashes on a beach on Vancouver Island, in a kitchen on the Sechelt Peninsula sewing a quilt from indigo linen she's dyed on a cedar bench by her garden while pileated woodpeckers teach their young to fly nearby. Her (my) own children have flown but she remembers them on the trail down to the school bus, shadowed by the dog whose pelvic bone sits on her desk, a reminder of injury, recovery, and the precarious nature of our lives.

The essay is having a moment. Or perhaps more accurately it's come into the light as a lively mutating organism. There are so many anthologies and workshops and gatherings devoted to its various forms and hybrids. There's even a sort of taxonomy that attempts to classify its shifting and capricious nature. The lyric essay. The hermit crab essay. The ekphrastic, the concrete, and on it goes. My nature, my writing nature, is drawn to what grows outside the boundaries. I've never followed a pattern to make a quilt and most of the meals I cook are versions of something, specific to place and time. Having said that, I have to say that I do read both quilt books and cookbooks. I read them like novels for what they can tell me about character and narrative, the influences of time.

These essays attempt to gather information: genealogies, medical histories and procedures, systems of music, colour theory, horticulture, methods of textile production, and early land surveys, among other things; the essays braid and weave and assemble patterns. I can't promise that any of this is entirely accurate or verifiable, though my intention is never to simply prevaricate or to use material deceptively. My interests do lie in the rich textures and possible meanings of the materials and how ostensibly scientific or quantifiable data can be repurposed in service to curiosity and to love, to undertake a deep investigation that might not otherwise be possible.

• • • • • •

My essays are mindful of the company they keep. Kathleen Jamie, the late Ellen Meloy, Ian Maleney, Anne Carson, Sinéad Gleeson, Peter Sanger, Lorri Neilsen Glenn, Brian Dillon, Lloyd Ratzlaff, Jane Silcott, Anik See, Rick Bass, and Maggie Nelson, among others: they've published celebrated collections of essays that use the form in creative and innovative ways. I read and I listen for how their sentences move across the page, a path forming in their wake. I am there, my own sentences following, joining them briefly, then meandering off the path to take the view from a small rise in a field, edged by a marsh. I tie a thread to a branch to remember my place. There are birds singing. Listen! A yellow-headed blackbird in the reeds by the water—! A tree hanging its leafy boughs over a slow creek where trout idle and the sky is reflected blue in the clear water. Dragonflies hover. I spread out the small quilt my grandmother made for my brother, patches of her housedresses and my grandfather's pyjamas. Pause with me, lie on your back in the soft grass. Human thought in real time. Sometimes the mind sleeps and the essay lies quietly beside it, waiting. Sometimes the mind walks tentatively into a cave and runs its fingers along a damp wall, a spiral of ochre dots, a long-horned aurochs, a horse paused in profile. In the far distance, my grandchildren are turning cartwheels, my husband of more than forty years is dreaming of the months he spent planning the rooflines of our house. You are welcome here. Anyone who has followed the thread this far knows what I mean.

A Dark Path

To get back up to the shining world from there
My guide and I went into that hidden tunnel;
And following its path, we took no care
To rest, but climbed: he first, then I—so far,
Through a round aperture I saw appear
Some of the beautiful things that Heaven bears,
Where we came forth, and once more saw the stars.
    —THE INFERNO OF DANTE[1]

IN THE NIGHT I was sitting at my desk thinking about Dante.
I woke after midnight and came downstairs, feeling my way with bare
feet. My husband and I have begun to read *The Inferno*, one canto at a
time in front of our woodstove each evening after dinner. The cantos
are full of dark woods, animals, poets, guides, the circles of Hell,
unfortunate souls tormented for eternity by fire, burning rivers of
blood, and mud.

In the dark, with the desk lamp and its small light:
What are you afraid of?
Because it was fear that kept me from sleeping.

I was thinking about Dante in a room shadowy with lamplight. Outside, a pair of coyotes circling each other in readiness to mate. I heard the female yip her fertility. Last week I saw a wolf walking on a gravel road leading up the mountain from the highway. We were driving, and as we passed, it stopped and turned to watch us. I saw its high hips, its long face. One morning, early, we were awake and heard wolves singing quite near. At least three voices, maybe more. It might have been that wolf with the rest of its pack.

What are you afraid of?

I am more than midway through my life's journey, like Dante as he entered the woods. I don't expect to meet a Virgil to guide me. Instead I will sew my way, using scraps of blue cloth, grey cloth, fine silks embroidered with forest flowers, setting each stone on a bed of thin muslin, careful of my footing. Two months ago I fell on an icy side-walk, and I fractured my coccyx; the impact resulted in a torn retina and dull pain encircling my pelvic girdle. Sitting, I am reminded of the dangers of uncertain paths. Walking, I put one foot carefully in front of the other. I am practising weekly in water to balance my move-ments so that I will be less likely to fall again. But I'm more than midway through the journey.

• • • • • •

When our dog Lily died in 1996, we brought her body home from the vet and thought about where we'd bury her. She was a large Lab–Shepherd cross, with a little wolf in her past. You could see it in her body, in her face. And in her wild nature. She was happy to be part of our pack, but she wouldn't be trained in the usual way. If it made sense to her to come when we called, then she would. If she was doing something else, something more important to her, then she wouldn't.

Anyway, she was big. The thought of digging a hole in rocky ground for her body was daunting. But John found a place in the woods, a deep hollow, with cedars all around. He cleared out a space for Lily's body, lined it with moss, and carried her there in the wheel-barrow. He covered her with a thick layer of moss. Then he cut branches of cedar, salal, and heaped them over the top.

A couple of years later, I went to the place and pushed the branches and moss aside. I could see a clean skeleton in the hollow. I reached in, removed a section of bone I quickly realized was Lily's pelvis, and brought it into the house. I soaked it for a few days in mild bleach solution and dried it off. I wanted something of her on my desk. In those years, my children were growing up so quickly, and I knew they'd be leaving soon. In fact, the oldest had already gone away to school, and I missed him terribly. I knew our family was changing, and I wanted a physical anchor to the years when we camped in the summers, Lily with us, the nights sweet and star-filled.

Sometimes people would see the bone on my desk and wonder at it. When I explained what it was, I could tell that most of them thought it was macabre to keep a dog's pelvis at hand. But it was beautiful, the clean bone smooth as ivory. And how different is it to keep antlers or actual ivory? Both share a collagen matrix, though ivory has no system of blood vessels. Thirty-five thousand years ago, people were making representative figures from bone and ivory—Venuses, horses, reindeer—and also had shrines to the dead that included bones. I'm not making a case for fetishizing my dog's pelvis. I just wanted to have something of her to look at every day. To remember her strong body, her high hips.

Perhaps eight years ago, I was in the kitchen and I heard a loud crash. It came from my study. We had no household animals at that time. Had a bird or some other creature come in through an open door and knocked something heavy to the floor? (Once, a weasel found its way in and raced around the house, running up a wall of books and along the top of a window, until we were able to shoo it out with a broom.) Investigating, I saw that a high shelf erected above the big window in my study, the width of the small room, had fallen, bringing its cargo of reference books (*Early Greek Myth*, *The Landmark Herodotus*, *Cruden's Concordance*, *Bartlett's Familiar Quotations*), an elk skull, and an old bean crock from my parents' house down onto my desk. My little desk lamp was broken. A geode had cracked in half. And Lily's pelvis was broken too, fractured from the point of the ischiatic arch along the line of the symphysis pubis and ischii; the entire sacrum had broken away.

Crack. CRACK.

I thought about putting it back together with some sort of glue. Maybe hot glue? Or the kind of adhesive we used to install ceramic tiles on our counters. But I never did. Sometimes I'd take up the three parts and fit them as they'd been before their fracture. It was interesting to run my finger along the hard compact bone on the outside edge; it resembled ivory. Within, the cancellous bone looked like fine dry sponge, containing what was left of the marrow. Lily's pelvis had cradled her bladder, some of her intestines, and, originally, her reproductive organs, before her ovaries and uterus were removed when she was young, before she came to us.

The desk lamp was repaired with duct tape. And now, more than twenty years after Lily's death, I am holding her pelvis in my hands, thinking about how long a life is, and how brief. What vanishes and what remains.

• • • • • •

What are you afraid of?

It's a disembodied voice, asking out of thin air.

A sentry at the gates of Elsinore. The voice of Bernardo, *Who's there?*[2]

It's dark, mid-winter, and I am awake, aware of uncertainties in the night around me. In my bed I am holding my knees to my chest, trying to alleviate the pain in my coccyx.

And then Francisco, *Nay, answer me. Stand and*
unfold yourself.

I wouldn't say I'm afraid, exactly. But something is changing. My
relationship to my body, the way the days are measured out now in
increments I need to think about, because how many of them are left?

Some of the fabric scraps I'm using for the path are decades old.
A little length of indigo cotton from Japan, from a package of sample
pieces, a small gift to myself perhaps thirty years ago. Deep blue
linen cut from a larger scrap brought home from a store on Granville
Island where I bought my first container of indigo powder for dyeing.
A barrel of linen offcut from the clothing that same store created for
those who could afford such luxurious attire, a sign reading, *Fill a*
bag, 10 dollars, and the bags were big paper ones. These are my years,
scraps of my years, cut into squares and small rectangles, arranged
as a series of cobbles for the mind to step along, carefully, one after
another.

When I was a young mother of one, I made a short path to our
outhouse, the first structure we built as we cleared a site and planned
our house. The building code required that you have an outhouse. Or
did it? I know that something called a perc test was necessary: we dug
three big holes to determine the water absorption rate of the soil in
the area where the septic field would be constructed. And I think one
of those was the hole we built our outhouse around, a small plywood
structure with a shed roof and a door with a quarter-moon cut-out
covered with screen to prevent mosquitoes. I put my baby on a blanket
nearby and used a heavy pick to etch a winding path leading to the
outhouse door, switching between the sharp end and the chiselled
end to break up the rough earth. I searched for flat rocks to set into the
path, fitting them together as firmly as I could, and I planned to grow
some creeping thyme between the rocks. I used a sledgehammer on
some, trying to crack them open for a smooth surface to face up from
the ground. I was young, I lifted the heavy hammer, and I brought it
down with force.

Crack. (Some rocks crumbled, others opened like a seam.)

It gave me pleasure to step on the rocks as I walked to the outhouse. But that path has long disappeared back into the ground, settled, grown over with grass and moss. And the outhouse was moved farther away after it was no longer needed, the hole filled in, and now it's a shed for chainsaw gas, kerosene for the lamps we use when the power goes out, and various other combustibles we don't want to store near the house.

Stand and unfold yourself.

When I fell and cracked my tailbone, I couldn't get up for what seemed like hours but was probably five or eight minutes. I sat on the frozen sidewalk, my suitcase behind me where the handle had dropped from my mittened hand. Was anything broken? I didn't know yet. The path to the Airbnb was scraped clear of snow and when I was able to stand, unfolding my body from its crumpled state on a public sidewalk, I hobbled along as carefully as I could, pulling my suitcase. My back hurt and my chest hurt where the wind had been knocked out of me. I hadn't expected to fall. I wasn't prepared to be injured. I was wearing good snow boots and my warmest jacket.

As I was piecing together the dark path, the frozen sidewalk south of the river in Edmonton, I thought of the stone path to the outhouse; the trail to beaches I've loved in my sixty-four years, draped with snowberry, thimbleberry, black hawthorn, and ninebark; the trail through salal and Oregon grape, created as a shortcut for my children's daily walk, accompanied by Lily, to where the school bus stopped for them on its way from Egmont to their schools, now overgrown. Sometimes I see Lily waiting at the top of the trail—waiting in sunlight, in rain, in snow—for the sound of the bus gearing down on its way back, waiting to greet them and guide them home.

Such was the footing we had down that ravine—
And at the broken chasm's edge we found
The infamy of Crete

Up the trail to the top of Mount Daniel. Walk the moon rings where
girls learned to be women and where you understand something
about eternity in the way the sky goes on, the way water carries boats
down the strait. And closer, the voices carrying over the finger of bay
directly below. On that trail Lily stumbled, tore her cruciate ligament,
limped slowly down in front of us (and we, in deference to her dignity,
followed just as slowly), but alert as ever, for bears, the stealthy feet of
cougars in the underbrush. The trail twisted and turned, dark as night
under the trees, opening to brilliant light, then shaded again. Going
up felt like rising to the top of the world; descending was

a rubble of scattered stone
That shifted under me often as I walked,

led by a black dog down the mountain to deep water, a dog whose
years were numbered, as mine are. I am counting as I write this,
as I plan ways to finish the textile that records the rubble, the solid
footwork, and what disappears.

· · · · · ·

We passed *The Inferno* back and forth, the space between us an arm's
length at most. Folded into our chairs on a winter's evening, the fire
warm, our glasses of wine a comfort. Sometimes the poem was a
foreign thing, so taken up with the saved and the righteous, and sometimes, oh, it spoke true to my heart, to the thing at hand, the fabrics,
the beautiful sashiko needles from Japan, the snipped lengths of deep
blue embroidery silk for stitching.

That path of stones
Would not provide a road for those who wore

Lead mantles, for we—he weightless, I helped up—
Could barely make our way from spur to spur.

We were swimming to regain our old bodies, the ones lithe and
flexible. In water we had no weight, my husband's hip lost its sore
clicking, my old injury and my new one were as though they'd never
happened. Stroke up and down the long blue pool, stroke, glide, turn
in the water, until it's time to walk on land again, feet uncertain on
the uneven surface.

• • • • • •

Some days my hands are so cold when I thread my fine needles, look
for the best way to sew my path together from its fragments of wool,
silk, linen, cotton. A jug of forced yellow forsythia on the table, a draft
from where the kitchen floor steps up to the living room, air drawn
from the dark space under the house. Now and then, a lighter scrap to
contrast with the indigos, the intense blues, and intricate prints. One
hand smoothing, the other easing the needle in and out, its tail of blue
thread following.

• • • • • •

I wasn't afraid that day when I was fourteen and I saddled my horse,
a black Anglo-Arabian gelding, to ride with a couple of friends in a big
open field behind our home in Victoria. It was windy. It was almost
Halloween.

I remember my friends were letting their horses gallop up a long
slope, but my horse was hot, he hadn't been ridden for a few days,
and I didn't want to give him his head. I remember him rearing, and
I remember him losing his balance, and then he was coming down in
a sitting position on my lap. My feet were still in the stirrups.

(Crack.)

It's so long ago. What do I truly remember? My horse raced away.
I was left on the ground, on my back, winded. Someone had been

watching from the houses beyond the field. *Are you hurt? Can you get up?* I didn't know. Could I? I don't remember pain.

An ambulance came. I was taken to the hospital and X-rayed. My pelvis was fractured.

(*Crack.*)

It was a long process, the healing of my pelvis. A month in hospital and then a transfer to a rehabilitation centre so I could learn to walk again, my leg muscles useless after a month on my back unable to use them. When I could finally stand, after the month of intensive exercise, in water, on parallel bars, with weights on my ankles, with the hand of a blind physiotherapist groping my crotch as he directed me to lift first one leg then another (and in memory I couldn't imagine anyone believing that he would do this; how would he even know where to place his hand, I imagined them saying, this man whom everyone revered like a saint), anyway, when I could finally stand, I felt dizzy and not quite of this world.

Who's there?

I remember being able to take short walks on my own, along paths threaded through rhododendrons and holly, adjacent to the Gorge Waterway, and coming back to the life I knew, but as a changed person. I was afraid, yes, afraid, of leaving the protected sanctuary of the rehabilitation centre, the other women in my room with their broken hips and paralyzed limbs, their stories, the sounds they made in the night as they dreamed, their lives circumscribed, as mine was, by the schedules of healers and those bringing our meals to our bedsides. Afraid of who I needed to become to carry myself into the future with the memory of a black horse falling onto me, a blind man's hands reaching for my pubis, the scent of winter on the dark paths I walked on my uncertain legs. *Stand and unfold yourself*, said Francisco.

*(Crack, oh tender pelvic girdle, healed, healed, supporting the
weight of the upper skeleton, transferring weight to the lower skeleton
during movement, protecting the organs I would need and use to become
a mother, healed but never without the faint line of a crack.)*

Ten years after that fracture, expecting my first child, I asked my
new doctor if he could send for the X-rays and determine whether the
old fracture would mean difficulties in carrying a baby to term. I don't
think he showed me the X-ray, but he identified the fracture as having
been to the pubic symphysis, the joint connecting the two sides of
the pelvis. He felt I'd been young enough at the time of the accident
that the joint would have healed well. Hormones released during
pregnancy would help the cartilage supporting the joint to become
flexible, to facilitate the delivery of the baby.

• • • • • •

Looking now at Lily's pelvis on my desk, I can see that the injury it
suffered when the heavy shelf fell on it was where my own pelvis was
fractured, a shared symmetry. I hold her broken bones in my hands,
running my thumb along the fine dry sponge of the cancellous, fitting
the seam together again and holding it in place. She never gave birth.
I had three children pass through my pelvis into the world, my body
a path for them into their own lives, a path of sunlight and darkness,
narrow, the passage difficult at times, opening.

> Some of the beautiful things that Heaven bears,
> Where we came forth, and once more saw the stars.

A path of rocks, some of them split open with a young woman's
strength, has long since returned to earth, hidden under decades of
grass and moss, perhaps faintly detected by bare toes on a summer
morning. And the trail from childhood to lives in the beautiful
damaged world—knitted back together by salal, bramble, shaded by
cedars, faint voices of those children heard when the light is right, the
heart ready to hear them. A path down a mountain with an injured

guide, no poet but a dog gone to memory. Scraps of fabric hoarded for years, held to the window, cut into approximations of rectangles, and pieced, waiting for me to join the seams together to make a whole. Dark blues, greys, silks from India embroidered with flowers and sequined, a small length of indigo printed with saffron moons. *Unfold yourself.* Unfold the path made of pieced fragments, broken geometries.

I didn't expect Dante to guide me back to my adolescence, saddling a black horse on a windy day, nor to an arrangement of smooth pale bones on my desk, something once whole now fractured into three parts. Nor did I expect a cobbled length of patchwork to walk me back to a girl and a dog. In the dark, with the desk lamp and its duct tape and its small light, I am surrounded by the night. I am listening for wolves. I'm not afraid.

The Blue Etymologies

blue (bloo), a. Of the colour between green and violet in the spectrum, coloured like the sky or deep sea (also of things much paler, darker, etc., as smoke, distant hills, moonlight, bruise...)[1]

WHEN ISAAC NEWTON passed white light through a prism in the seventeenth century, he saw a rainbow. He concentrated his attention on seven colours, to correlate with the seven notes on a musical scale, the seven days of the week. His analogy was interesting but tells us more about the nature of light than about music and colour, or how we organize time. Still, I remember a song we learned in elementary school choir about colour; we sang a rainbow. We listened with our eyes and sang everything we saw, looking at the arc of colours on the blackboard chart.

How would it sing back, that rainbow? Red, *do*; orange, *re*; yellow, *mi*; green, *fa*; blue, *so*; indigo, *la*; violet, *ti*: all the way back to *do*. Think of your hands on the piano keys. Think of a violin scale. A harp. Think of a calendar, ringing its days, its sequences of hours.

Looking out the window, while singing, a child might see a blue sky; this is due to a complicated optical illusion called the Rayleigh scattering, the scattering of light off the air's molecules. Those classrooms of my childhood were high-ceilinged, they smelled of

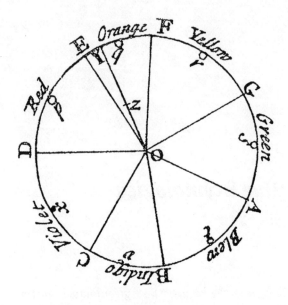

Newton's Colour Wheel, ca. 1665. [Isaac Newton, Opticks, *4th ed., 1730, Wikimedia Commons]*

apple cores and chalk, and wool mittens steaming on radiators. There was also a boy who could fart the opening bars of "O Canada" and was encouraged to do this often by a coterie of other boys who were loud with their praise and who, I suspect, practised the skill at home or among themselves without such impressive results. I used to sit at my desk, waiting until we could read. The first readers, *Tales of Dick and Jane*, were too simple but once I could prove I could read every word, I was allowed to choose a book to take to my desk, while my classmates sat in a circle and followed the antics of Baby Sally, one slow syllable at a time. *Blue Willow* is the one I remember best. A girl whose family riches were almost non-existent, apart from a platter in the blue willow pattern; it was lost once, for reasons to do with greed and cruelty, and it was recovered, to adorn a mantel in a simple house where the young protagonist and her family live happily ever after. I read the book again and again. I wished for such a platter in our house where Melmac was the tableware and something with bullrushes the pattern. The food served on those plates always tasted slightly soapy, because my mother washed dishes earnestly but never rinsed them.

Think of your hands on the piano keys. (Listen with your eyes.) Or on top of your desk while the teacher explained long division or the meaning of Canada. I spent a lot of time studying the veins on the backs of my hands instead of paying attention to the rules of long division. Mine were deep blue, almost grey, the colour of the lead sinkers in my father's fishing tackle box. I'd turn my hands up, then down, watching the veins swell, then empty, as the blood moved from my hands to my heart. I'd tap them. I'd kiss them, if I knew no one was looking. Many years later, I found the moment in Act II, Scene 5 of *Antony and Cleopatra*:

> ...and here
> My bluest veins to kiss, a hand that kings
> Have lipped, and trembled kissing.

Of course no one had kissed my veins, my hands, no one but me, pressing my mouth to the lead-blue swellings. (In later years, I'd linger, imagining a mouth against my own, imagining lips with the texture of my hands.) But the room smelled of apple cores and chalk and cabbagey farts, not a haven for a girl who spent her time in wonder. A blue willow platter, the soft skin of my own hands, a few tattered books on the windowsill of the classroom.

• • • • • •

Where does blue come from, what does it mean? I ask myself the questions and my answers are personal, deeply subjective. I'm not alone in my attraction to blue. Maybe we love it because our blue mind loves the ocean (though Homer described it as "wine-dark," possibly alluding to its pellucid qualities rather than its colour), a clear sky: we want our world to be clean and untainted. A string of azurite beads thumbed on the wrist as a way to cleanse thinking, to focus the inner eye.

After a dinner party, I wash a new cloth for the first time, rinsing out the small spills of juices from the casserole, some splashes of red wine. The cloth is block-printed cotton, dark indigo, printed with white leaves. I bought it at a pop-up shop in the Masonic Hall in Roberts Creek, choosing it from dozens of possible tablecloths folded on a table in the middle of the room. I could smell its dye. Probably not indigo—synthetic dyes have largely replaced the traditional compounds of madder, turmeric, henna, teak tree, and acacia bark— but then when I hang it to dry, my hands are stained blue. I leave them blue on purpose, to remind me of the months ahead when my own dye vat will be placed on a bench created by a felled cedar, boards sliced from it until the core was left.

• • • • • •

> **ME ▸b** Livid, leaden-coloured (esp. Of the skin as a result of cold, fear, etc.). **ME ▸c** Of a flame or flash: without red glare. **L16**[2]

When I began to make quilts, in 1987, I wanted to explore blue. A soft patchwork of pale blue prints worked into Ohio stars paired with unbleached cotton; a composition of log-cabin blocks, blue strips, and yellow ascending in shade from a tiny square of red, for the hearth, in the middle of the block; red tulips in a haze of forget-me-nots. I began to think of ways to print the surfaces myself, with wax resist and clamps and strands of tough string. I batiked leaping salmon and then drew thread through the cloth in the mokume shibori technique, pulling it tight and knotting it. The waxed and tied bundles were immersed in a deep blue Procion dye. Before taking them out and rinsing them, I cracked the wax a little to allow dye to penetrate the resisting fish. Once I'd removed all the wax, using my mother's old iron and many pages of newspaper, I liked the results, though the lines of mokume weren't as wavery as I'd hoped they would be. I had some fabric paint and used a fine brush to detail the salmon with lines of red along the tail and fins. I loved what Yoshiko Iwamoto Wada wrote in *Memory on Cloth: Shibori Now*:

> When the cloth is returned to its two-dimensional form, the design that emerges is the result of the three-dimensional

shape, the type of resist, and the amount of pressure exerted by the thread or clamp that secured the piece during the cloth's exposure to the dye. The cloth sensitively records both the shape and the pressure; it is the "memory" of the shape that remains imprinted in the cloth. This is the essence of shibori.[3]

You do this for the process and what you learn along the way. That waxed dental floss sewn along lines with a basting stitch can be pulled tight for water, that waxing a fish into plain cotton with a mixture of paraffin and beeswax, then dipping the cotton in blue dye gives you a memory of watching coho spawn in the creek near your house, a cycle that has been going on since the last ice age at least. That others have dipped cloth into dye and worn the pigment on their hands for weeks afterwards.

When I did this work, I remembered another occasion, outside, taking lengths of linen out of the tray where they'd been setting overnight after a morning of frequent timed immersions. While I was doing this, I realized the sound I was hearing, agitated, loud, was a whole family of pileated woodpeckers, the young having just learned to fly. They were flapping around awkwardly and making the most comical noise while the parents scolded and encouraged. Mosquitoes kept stinging the small of my back. What the cloth remembers, I will remember too—gathering the stones, sewing the circles that became the growth rings of larch, tying cotton string as tightly as I could. And the cloth and I will also remember the raucous sound of adolescent pileated woodpeckers finding their wings, learning what a voice sounds like in open air, in the morning, before the heat begins.

Weeks later, sewing spirals that draw together three layers of cloth—the newly dyed surface, cotton batting in-between, and a back of old sheets or muslin—I try to recall each step of the process: filling the vat and measuring indigo, additives, finding a long cedar stick to stir the bundles of tied, clamped, and bundled cloth, brushing mosquitoes from my clothing, leaving streaks of blue on my old T-shirt, allowing the cloth to drip on the grass.

Maybe we are cloth, we are the very fabric of being, the world recorded on us like blue dye, the sound of woodpeckers echoing in the trees just beyond.

• • • • • •

Caught, blue-handed

Careless about gloves, I am caught blue-handed. My thumbs make a blue mark on paper. I have plunged tied and clamped fabric, some of it heavy with bound stones, into a vat of indigo dye. Stirred the lengths. Removed them so they could oxidize on a summer morning. Dipped again, many times, my gloves either too hot, or not long enough (blue-wristed, I manipulate bundles of stone-tied linen), and inevitably torn by the cedar stick I am using to stir. The bundles come out of the vat the colour of swamp water but darken to the deepest blue over the course of the morning's repeated dippings. While I stir, I watch Steller's Jays sail from trees to deck railings. They belong to the genus *Cyanocitta*, gathering the North American jays together. Κυάνεος, or Kuaneos, meaning "deep blue," combined with Kitta, or Kissa, meaning "jay." In Homeric times, Kuaneos was the deep blue easing to black, exactly the colour of a Steller's Jay, and oh, the colour I hope for as I dip my bundles repeatedly into a vat of indigo.

Colour is subjective and others might not see what I see when I dry my cloth (stones and string and wooden blocks removed) on the clothesline, gloves abandoned, so that my hands are damp blue as I peg up the lengths. It's not quite the blue of jays, or the blue of veiled Tuareg men, not the deep indigo of new Levi's. I love it but know that I'll have to try again for the blue I really aspire to, my thumbprint whorled and ridged on the edges where I've gripped before hanging up the cloth to dry in the sun. And later, printed again, on paper, as I make a note after washing my hands, the dye renewed by water. Marked by blue, as the twelfth-century artist applying lapis lazuli to a manuscript, shaping her brush with her lips repeatedly as she worked, is known to us now by the residues of pigment in the tartar of her teeth.[4]

A clothesline hung with indigo cloth, fresh from my dye vat.

• • • • • •

A recipe for indigo

2 a Taken as the colour of constancy. **LME** ▸**b** Taken as
the colour of sorrow or anguish (see also sense 3). **LME** ▸**c**
Taken as the colour of plagues and things hurtful. **E16**[5]

We'd only just arrived in Edmonton. I had new boots, Helly Hansen
winter ones, lined with shearling, and they had good soles. I drove our
rental car from the airport to the Airbnb just around the corner from
Brendan and Cristen's house. The plan was to drop off our suitcases
and then walk over to join them for dinner. The road was packed with
snow and I crossed so carefully. The sidewalk had been scraped clear,
though, and it seemed dry. Pulling my suitcase behind me, I strode
towards the house where our suite was waiting. Then I fell down.

Down as hard as I've ever fallen. I didn't see the patch of black ice and my feet, my legs, shot out in front of me. I can't remember the first minute or so. John was there, asking, Theresa, are you all right? And was I? I didn't know. I couldn't move. I couldn't catch my breath. My body was a single enormous pain.

Can you get up, you have to get up, John said gently, holding my arms. I turned over so that I was on my hands and knees. Could I get up? I didn't know. I almost couldn't move. But then I did. I walked slowly to the house and tried to assess what had happened, how I felt. I was in pain. My body was pain. But my legs worked. My arms. I'd caught my breath and closed my eyes to focus my breathing. Not my ribs, then. They allowed my lungs to expand and contract without hurting. But when I sat down on the chair by the door, my lower torso ached. So was it my tailbone? Fractured? Or just bruised?

But I could walk, so we gathered our stuff together and walked slowly over to the next street to have dinner with our family. It was wonderful to see them and I was tender with myself when I bent to hug the children, to sit down at the table to eat and laugh and hear the latest news. In turn, they were tender with me. Grandma is broken, my granddaughter told her younger brother.

It wasn't until three days later that the silver light began to fall to the right of my face, long beautiful streams of it. Mostly in a dark room (we were watching an abbreviated performance of *The Nutcracker* with our grandchildren), but then at other times, like in the bedroom when I was resting with the blinds closed to the bright snow. I also began to see small nests of fine twigs or hairs in my right eye, passing by. None of this was painful. But when I mentioned these experiences to my family, in our rented suite, panic ensued. My daughter, searching the internet, discovered information about potential retinal damage and wouldn't let me brush off any possible danger. My husband phoned hospitals—it was a Sunday afternoon—and he was advised to bring me to Emergency at the Royal Alexandra Hospital immediately. It was snowing. We drove across the Walterdale Bridge over a North Saskatchewan River white with ice forming, glittering, and the city north of the bridge blurred by snow.

My husband's hands were tight on the steering wheel and my son's voice was calm: At the next light, turn left. Make sure you get into the turning lane. Cars slid as they turned.

An emergency ward is a sad place to spend hours of time you could be with your grandchildren and their parents, enjoying a special dinner on your last night in Edmonton. People came in holding an arm in an improvised sling, a towel to a battered face, a sleeping child on a father's lap while the mother held a bucket to her mouth. The smell was wet wool and disinfectant.

When we saw the emergency room physician, he asked questions gently, kindly. He examined my eyes thoroughly and told us that he suspected that there was a posterior vitreous detachment with the danger of retinal detachment. He didn't believe the visual issues were a result of the fall. He was insistent that I needed to see a retinal specialist before flying home the next day at noon. He was going to make phone calls and see if he could pull some strings to get me an appointment early the next morning. (My husband had already alerted our travel insurance providers in the event we had to cancel our flight.) Leaving us for a time, the doctor returned with a big smile. He had discovered that an ophthalmology resident was currently upstairs in the Eye Institute and was willing to examine me immediately.

She was young and very thorough. She asked detailed questions and used various instruments to examine my eyes. Peering into my eye with a three-mirror lens, she suspected she was seeing a retinal tear but confessed that there was so much blood from a hemorrhage, its source obscured. Again, she didn't believe the fall was the reason I'd had visual problems. She too would be happier if I saw a specialist before leaving Edmonton but agreed that I could return home if I promised to see an ophthalmologist. I wasn't sure there was one on our part of the coast but I knew that there were optometrists and surely one of them could refer me on if needed. She would provide detailed notes of her examination for me to give to whomever I saw.

What I remember about her examinations: there was a moment when she was shining a bright light into the back of my eye and I saw a red desert landscape with long fissures transcribing it. I think this might have been what's called a Purkinje tree, the view of my own retinal blood vessels interpreted by my brain using a correlative image from its stored hoard. Which is why what I saw resembled a National Geographic photograph of a dry and cracked desert surface. I saw ochre earth and deep crevasses.

Then, as she moved her light, there was an intense blue sky with tumbling white clouds. It was the blue I've tried to find with indigo dye, timing the immersions and the following periods of oxidation in order to allow the dye to penetrate the fibres as deeply as possible. Although I've loved the results of my efforts, they were never as blue as I hoped for. But this sky, blue, *blue* in that room above the dark and snowy city, the clouds moving slowly as if by warm air currents.

When we returned home to the Sechelt Peninsula, I discovered that there are in fact two ophthalmologists practising in the small town forty-five minutes from our house. My doctor made an emergency appointment with one of them. First a technician performed some preliminary tests and while her light was shining into my right eye, I saw what seemed to be the retinal blood vessels. They were lines of red against a background of pink or ochre, veiny like I expected something in my body to be. This was not the sere desert scored by cracks I'd seen a few days earlier in Edmonton. Then the ophthalmologist studied the photographs the technician had put on a screen for him and he did a number of examinations with lights. You have a tear in your retina, he said. Just as the young resident had suspected. He was surprised that she'd seen it because there was an overlying hemorrhage that made it difficult to see. But definitely a tear. And it had to be repaired immediately, with lasers. Yes, he replied in answer to my question about the origins of the damage: this is almost certainly a result of your fall. You've had a trauma and your retina is damaged as a result. When I asked the ophthalmologist what I'd seen during that examination, he wrote down "entoptic phenomenon" on a piece of paper and I tucked it into my pocket.

Looking at the piece of paper later, after the drops to dilate my pupils, after the laser surgery, after the long drive home, my husband quiet and me reclined, my eyes closed, I parse the word "entoptic": from the Greek, εντός οπτικός or "within vision," i.e., vision within the eye itself. I read about blue field entoptic phenomenon or Scheerer's phenomenon, in which moving white dots are actually white blood cells flowing in the capillaries in front of the retina. Some people think that the experience is like seeing heaven, an aspect of consciousness, an apprehension of angels. I saw billowing clouds in the deepest blue sky, and the clouds were moving across the sky just as clouds move when one looks up for a sustained period at a summer sky. But my experience of that blue and its white clouds was brief. Brief, and as beautiful as anything I've ever seen. And it was within my eye, apprehended in the light of an ophthalmologist's instrument. When she removed the instrument, I was in an examining room in a high tower while snow whirled around the windows and the river froze under the bridge we would have to cross on our way home.

I learn that the silver light that fell to the periphery of my vision was caused by little waves in the vitreous jelly hitting the retina. The fall on ice had caused these coruscations. Sitting in the dark, at the Grindstone Theatre watching that abbreviated version of *The Nutcracker*, and lying in my dark room at the Airbnb, trying to ease the pain in my tailbone, it was as though I was seeing the summer meteor showers, the shimmer of light as the meteors entered the earth's upper atmosphere and burned up in a display of brilliance in the night.

I thought of the blue that my eye had conjured within itself, the colour I try to find through dyes and other pigments (the ceiling in the room where I am typing is a deep blue, as close to the Scrovegni ceiling painted by Giotto in the early fourteenth century, for which he used lapis lazuli ground and mixed with binding agents, as close to that blue as I could get, using a guidebook from the chapel and the scanner at the hardware store). I thought of the blue I dreamed, just out of reach when I woke next morning, and how I've tried to find ways of mixing it, recipes for it.

In Werner's *Nomenclature of Colours*,[6] we're told that "Indigo Blue, is composed of Berlin Blue, a little black, and a small portion of apple green." And Prussian blue? ("Beauty spot of wing on Mallard Drake.")

Well, it's "Berlin blue, with a considerable portion of velvet black, and a small quantity of indigo blue." And Berlin blue? ("Wing feathers of Jay.") "Berlin Blue, is the pure, or characteristic colour of Werner. W." Who was Werner, you ask? He was Abraham Gottlob Werner (1749–1817), a mineralogist and geologist born in Prussian Silesia who developed a scheme for identifying minerals by key characteristics. His work was furthered by Patrick Syme (1774–1845) who extended Werner's charts to include natural history.

When you fall into the rabbit hole of pigments and how they were developed, you could tunnel down forever. You'd find the origins of Prussian blue, a story involving a toxic compound called Dippel's oil (created by its namesake as an alchemical attempt to make an elixir of immortality, containing crushed animal bones and blood) accidentally added to a vat of red dye composed of crushed insects, iron sulphate, and potash. The result was a colour that the world was waiting for and embraced with such enthusiasm that it was used for everything from colouring tea to military uniforms to the palette of Picasso where it inspired his Blue Period. Berlin blue, slight variant of the pigment, was manufactured in China and exported to Japan where it appeared as the key colour of Hokusai's beautiful views of Mount Fuji, in part because of its ability to lend depth to sky and water.

• • • • • •

The blue hour, the one we wait for in late February when the sun slips down below the horizon and the sky deepens to the saturated indigo of a Maxfield Parrish landscape, a platter of truite au bleu on the long table, a glass of Modrý Portugal poured and waiting on the counter. An hour to be accompanied by the music of Miles Davis, Joni Mitchell. Stitch, stitch the dyed linen into rough quilts, spread the Indian cloth on the grass for the evening picnic, your hands blue with cold.

• • • • • •

> *I have walked behind the sky.*
> —DEREK JARMAN[7]

I had long wanted to see "true" indigo, and thought that drugs
might be the way to do this. So one sunny Saturday in 1964,
I developed a pharmacologic launchpad consisting of a base of
amphetamine (for general arousal), LSD (for hallucinogenic
intensity), and a touch of cannabis (for a little added delirium).
About twenty minutes after taking this, I faced a white wall and
exclaimed, "I want to see indigo—now!"

And then, as if thrown by a giant paintbrush, there appeared
a huge, trembling, pear-shaped blob of the purest indigo.
Luminous, numinous, it filled me with rapture. It was the color
of heaven...
—OLIVER SACKS[8]

It hadn't occurred to me that a person could summon indigo other
than by mixing colour. My own recipe for producing it is pretty tame.
Indigo powder (which is sourced from a farm in India, not grown in
my garden and fermented in a vat), thiourea dioxide, lye, Synthrapol
soap, and soda ash. I use vinegar for rinsing the dyed fabrics. Some of
these are caustic but none, as far as I know, is capable of generating
hallucinations.

Would I use a cocktail of hallucinogens to see that inner sky
again? Would I mix a little of my precious vial of homemade cannabis
tincture (Texada Timewarp buds soaked in Silent Sam vodka) with
something else more powerful if it meant I could look upon that
cracked red desert beyond my irises? See the rich sky within my own
eye again? An inner landscape entirely my own? ("I have walked
behind the sky," wrote Derek Jarman.) I don't know. But I would be
in good company, including Dr. Sacks—and as I discover, reading
further on the phenomenon, those who entered caves perhaps 35,000
years ago to paint horses, bison, ibex, a gallery of lions, their own
hands outlined in unhydrated hematite.

Éliette Brunel, the smallest, physically, of the trio who first found
the Chauvet cave in the Ardèche region of France and thus the
one who led the others, entered the narrow passage into the cave
and cried out, "They have been here!"[9] Imagine that scene: a dark

gallery, a woman following a pair of red lines to arrive face to face with animals drawn in charcoal on rock, the dizzy moment when she realized the six chambers of panels amounted to something so vast and spectacular that it would change lives, alter the way artists and culture had been interpreted, dated, theorized. That people—men and women, an adolescent girl who left her handprint in red ochre—returned and returned to a cold space under the earth to leave a story for those who came after. They came in fear, in joy, and some left their own marks, dragging fingers wet with pigment along the rock surfaces as they descended.

To locate a place and to mark it with images so close to gods that they breathe still, after 30,000 years, or longer...this impulse, the shudder in the shoulders as the shapes appear out of the darkness at the tips of your fingers, your charcoal or ground pigments so carefully prepared: is this what we hope too with our powders and threads, our jar of ink, of leaves made into paste? When I hang our new cloth on a line in sunlight and press my face to its beauty? Breathing in the swampy scent of indigo, heady as grass clippings, oxygen, while above me the blue sky arches over the world. The cloth is a tent to hold me damp inside it.

> Colour the little wall maps of the universe you are making. The sapphire colour for the spheres of the world. It would be useful not just to look at it, but to reflect on it in the soul. Deep inside your house you might set up a little room and mark it with these figures and colours.[10]

Though it was thought to be frivolous at first to propose that the caves were sacred sites where shamanistic rituals were enacted, now many archaeologists believe that the nonrepresentational elements, as well as more representational recording of animals in beautifully dynamic ways, in paleolithic cave art are a form of entoptic phenomenon, induced by psychotropic plants. Traces of opium, cannabis seed, fermented barley, and other hallucinogens have been found in the teeth of those who may have been the sacred artists, in ceremonial bowls, and in bone tubes used to take in substances to induce trance states that probably resulted in imagery that remained consistent for more than 25,000 years: lattices, spirals, zigzag lines, filigrees, parallel lines. Our brains are hard-wired to see these images under certain circumstances, induced by drugs or by (as in my own case) an injury to the retina.

> The exact way in which entoptic phenomena are "wired into" the human nervous system has been a topic of recent research. It has been found that the patterns of connections between the retina and the striate cortex (known as VI) and of neuronal circuits within the striate cortex determined their geometric form (Bressloff et al., 2000). Simply put, there is a spatial relationship between the retina and the visual cortex; points that are close together on the retina lead to the firing of comparably placed neurons in the cortex. When this process is reversed, as following the ingestion of psychotropic substances, the pattern in the cortex is perceived as a visual percept. In other words, people in this condition are seeing the structure of their own brains.[11]

On a snowy evening in Edmonton, I sat in a chair high above the city glittering below, and saw images so beautiful that I know why people have sought them since they first ate datura or drank fermented honey and ingested mushrooms so toxic they could not have lived long afterwards. In dark caves they applied ochre, charcoal, and ground calcite to show light falling from the faces of horses and spiral patterns that led them to a dizzy apprehension of time and starlight. Following the spiral, they went to the heart of the mystery. It was never ours. It was always ours.

When I sew my spirals, I am finding my way into darkness, hopeful that I will find my way back. I am walking a path worn to the bare earth. It's one way I know to hear myself think. I sew small shell buttons to the ends of each trail, a place-marker, shining as the light shone by my face in an Edmonton room where I lay in intense pain, but also in joy as I heard my grandchildren singing: Two little dicky birds sitting on a wall, one named Peter, the other named Paul.

I remember the silver light falling beside my face, like the tails of shooting stars, in the dark cave of my bed at night, fearful and blessed, and how I will try to replicate that sensation—not just the visual beauty but the awe—in some way for the rest of my life. You dodged a bullet, the ophthalmologist told me, after a follow-up visit to make sure the retinal tear had healed, after he had shone lights for a second time and found a second tear, which he immediately repaired. You will always have these tears, he said, but the edges have been sealed with the lasers. He peered into each eye with a bright light. It was white with hope, it was as new as the beginning of the world.

We Are Still Here

J.S. Bach's Violin Partita No. 2 in D minor, BWV 1004

> *The leading British conductor and Bach scholar Christopher*
> *Hogwood, who in 1973 founded the Academy of Ancient Music*
> *with its mission to play Baroque music on period instruments, tells*
> *me that he's puzzled by students coming his way who, for instance,*
> *play minuets every day of their lives without knowing how to dance*
> *a minuet.*
>
> —PHILIP CLARK[1]

1 | *Allemanda, in Toulouse, on Mount Tolmie*

The opening, grave and ominous.

My mother has been dead for seven years. I've been researching family history—hers, in part; though mostly my father's mother's origins in Horni Lomná, in what's now the Czech Republic. Most days I find myself thinking about the strange and wonderful cartography of motherhood, across seas and generations, the maps imaginary and remote. How *my* mother's mother was unknown to her—my mum was given up at birth to a foster home and raised to think of herself as motherless—and how that first terrible loss shaped her, blank area on the map. She told a granddaughter once that she'd only ever wanted to

Mother and fawn at the edge of my property.

be a mother, as though she needed to fill the emptiness of herself with that function, scribble her place in geography. When I was young, it never seemed enough to me. I wanted more of her, from her. But now I realize—too late—what she gave me and my brothers.

In Toulouse, last March, I dreamed of my mother. I'd been thinking a great deal about geographical loneliness. Not only for a place one has left, often forever (my grandmother never returned to Europe and as far as I know, she had only very sporadic contact with her family there), but also the loneliness we feel when we try to follow the traces our ancestors left across a landscape. A map, on paper or in memory, a field loved by a child for its birdsong, the scent of plum blossom after a long winter, a tree planted to celebrate a wedding, a birth, an occasion long-forgotten. So the dream of my mother surprised me. She was on a guided tour, just before heart surgery. I always wanted to travel to France, she said, her eyes glowing as she jostled and joked with her new friends, but no one would ever go with me. She had photographs—a long road pink with oleander leading down to the sea, a restaurant filled with sunlight, a plate of sausage. (As far as I know, she never used a camera.) I held her hand and thought, I have another chance. We went to the restroom together and she was running. Please, Mum, don't run, I pleaded with her, only half in fun. Please. I don't want you to die on me!

(Walk three steps, then lift a foot. 2/4 time.)

Now I wish I'd offered to take her to France, though I wonder if she truly wanted to go or if the dream came from my own pleasure at the sight of umbrella pines, orange trees, the silvery leaves of olives. She confessed once, after my father died, that she'd always hoped to go to Greece. I looked at her with such surprise, I remember, because the trips she took were to Reno or Disneyland and once, to Hawaii. Packaged tours, on buses or charter flights. Later she and my father travelled to places he'd been to in the navy and insisted she'd love: Singapore, Hong Kong, Thailand. I don't think she did love those trips but my father was persuasive.

I have a photo album sent to her after her foster sister died. Mostly it's a record of her foster sister's life but there are a few early photographs of my mum, aged three, in a garden, or standing by some stairs. She is chubby and dark-haired. So far away in time, in geography—she grew up in Halifax. But somehow curiously present, her clear eyes, her smile. ("Thou art thy mother's glass, and she in thee..."[2] Her eyes, in mine. Her knees, with that migrating pain. At the end of her life, she could barely walk.)

Until her death, I don't believe I ever danced an Allemanda. A linear movement in binary form. Walk three steps, then lift a foot. 2/4 time. Four couples, her children and their partners, promenading the length of her living room in an apartment on the slope of Mount Tolmie, entwining their arms, as one lifts a box of photographs (though none of France), another passes a load of her clothing (the cardigans, the polyester trousers, the tiny socks, a few threadbare nightdresses), and the remaining dancers keep their place in the movement. There is nothing French in the apartment, no music but what I hear in my head as I step, as I sort, as I turn, turn, the old harmonies returning.

From Toulouse, lift, lift, make a place in your arms for a mother who ran like a girl to rejoin her friends who waited in France, who watched deer make their own graceful steps below her window on Mount Tolmie, lace your arms with hers, turn, turn, towards her, away. Careful with your knees as you lift each foot, stand where she stood, 2/4 time, the years passing before the window, like the deer.

2 | *Corrente, BC Cancer Agency, 600 West 10th Avenue, Vancouver, with longing, with expectation*

Quick step through the generous doors, quick step to the right where the sign points to Functional Imaging. Quick, quick, while you can, while the notes are tied, delicate.

When I entered, there was silence. Four or five people on chairs, one in a hospital smock, one man with an elegant leather handbag holding his mother's hand. I was asked to briefly sit and then I was invited into a room where a technologist injected me with radioactive sugar to act as a tracer in my body. What music would you like, he asked as he covered me with a warm flannel blanket and dimmed the lights. And Bach was my request. Violin accompanied me for sixty minutes as I closed my eyes and thought about my life, the life I loved and that might be changing.

Step, three beats, tap your leg through the thin cotton of your hospital gown. Step, step, step.

Having heard the *Quirks and Quarks* show on meditation, I'm pretty sure I wasn't meditating. I thought of the Venus of Laussel, a limestone bas-relief sculpture I saw a few years ago in Bordeaux. She dates from 29,000 to 20,000 BCE and has traces of red ochre on her breasts and abdomen. When I saw her, I knew her. There's nothing fashionable about her body. She's full and abundant. She's one of a group of female figures from the Paleolithic period and although there's some debate about what she's holding—a horn of plenty? A

Venus of Laussel, carved between 29,000 to 20,000 years ago, in the Dordogne Valley.
[Wikimedia Commons. Creative Commons license, Attribution Share-Alike 3.0, https://commons.
wikimedia.org/wiki/File:Venus-de-Laussel-vue-generale.jpg]

symbol of a woman's lunar cycles (there are thirteen lines inscribed in the shape)?—I think it's clear that she's a fertility symbol. A woman who has likely borne children and has known good meals, who has probably even provided them, from her own body and her own ingenuity.

She was a good companion for me during that part of the procedure. And when I had to lie on the narrow plank and enter the long cylinder for the scan itself—it took twenty minutes—I closed my eyes and thought of her again. It helped immensely to have her present. I brought to my mind's eye my husband and my children, their partners, my three grandchildren. Then I visualized each of my books, their thirteen titles in lines across my inner vision. My eyelids fluttered with effort and I almost cried. I was afraid if I opened my eyes, I would be nothing. I would be someone with radioactive glucose in her body and possibly something worse. But the goddess, her face absent of features but her body so complex and whole, stayed with me the whole time, her horn in her right hand. My hand flexed in time.

I was still inside the cylinder, still as a person sleeping, or dead. Eyes closed, mind filled with the beauty of my family, the binary forms I'd grown in my body, two sons, a daughter, each of them in turn born with undeveloped sperm or egg cells, contributions to the grandchildren who were oblivious to their grandmother still on a bench in the imaging scanner, their great-grandparents hovering too. And theirs. Impossibly light but all-powerful, prehistoric limestone, feathery penniform to her right, her wide buttocks and hips flaring, as mine flared under the blue cotton smock, my companion in the ceremonial cave where her horn was the thing that kept us steady together as we waited to learn if my cells were absorbing the glucose, if malignancies were hidden in my chest and torso.

The Venus gently pushed my foot to propel me back into the room, her hand surprisingly firm as it reached out of the stone, tapped her horn to my heels. There you are, go back! And when I came out of the cylinder, it was like being reborn. Sort of. I thought of John Berger's observations about the Chauvet Cave:

> Step outside the cave and re-enter the wind-rush of time passing. Reassume names. Inside the cave everything is present and nameless. Inside the cave there is fear, but the fear is in perfect balance with a sense of protection.[3]

Time now to take off the blue smock, put on your day clothes, two steps and then a double (single/single/double) to the left, then repeating the same to the right (heel blessed by the goddess), with single or double straight steps, a little skip as you leave the suite of rooms where you have been wrapped in warm flannel, sent into the cave (single, single, though your loved ones hovered). In the waiting room and the hall at the Cancer Agency you see the dancers moving slowly on the polished linoleum, two steps, a careful double, repeat, repeat, their wheelchairs and walkers, their canes and the arms of those who help to support them, the final bars of the Corrente slowed down, slow for those waiting for procedures, for leaving the imaging rooms, the rooms where the chemicals are dripped into veins, the beauty of the dance theirs for time suspended in the dust motes, "clearly music on which hopes are built,"[4] the bright lights overhead, the little groups huddled on benches, heads down in sorrow, hands clasped in fear.

3 | Sarabanda, from the Beskydy Mountains to old age on a porch in Edmonton

Stately, sweetly slow, take me there, one step, the stressed second.

A choreography of distance, a small wooden house in a tiny village in the Beskydy Mountains holding the girlhood of my father's mother, spruce trees along the road in front and the slope of the mountains behind. Fruit trees in snow. The sound of church bells. Plum blossom following the deep snow, the return of the sheep from sheds to the new grass. Stately slow, the ancient transhumance of sheep and their shepherds, a migration from one ridge of the Carpathians to the Beskydys, in snow, in sunlight. A poke in the ribs, slow, slow, the grazing, the arrivals in far pastures. As my grandmother walked, slow, with her children, one a baby wrapped in a shawl, in the snow on the road away from the village.

A slow triple, one step, a stressed second, age slowing the limbs in space, where is the foot, where is the knee that bent to potatoes, to the tiny chicks newly hatched, where is the arm in relation to the body, muscles firmed by laundry, the garden, rolling out dough for noodles she sold at the door, now gone. Gone the door, the batten walls. Where

The house where my grandmother was born—or so I believed when I first saw it.

is the photograph of Julia's funeral, chick grown to rooster, caught
by the camera, and children posed in the clothing they wore to Mass.
Where is the husband, dead also. And an earlier daughter, buried in
the cemetery above the town. Where.

Dust in summer. Cold wind off the river in winter. No one wanted
the work of potatoes, saving bags for dill seed, no one wanted to cut
noodles by hand when the market sold them in cellophane bags. Step,
step, slow as the melting of snow, the passing of time. In a chair on a
porch, tap your feet to old melodies, someone tuning a fiddle in a warm
room while the men drank slivovice and dreamed of making their
fortunes in the new world. The gypsies have come with their own strange
instruments, battered drums, a horn of burnished apricot wood, their
horses tied to the gate. The dancing that night was wild, every step

returned to its original intention. Kisses exchanged beyond the
firelight.

> It is as though some swift current of water swept you along
> with it.[5]

In Moravia, the small wooden house holds the memory of a daughter's feet on a bare floor, a daughter who waltzed out the door, with five small children, moved in the way a mother does, over the planks crossing the Lomná River, careful, careful—three steps, a foot lifted, the timing skewed as a child dropped a valise, another cried, and they danced a sweet Sarabanda together towards Jablunkov, then Antwerp, then Canada. They never saw Horni Lomná again.

On the porch, almost deaf, aging feet find the tempo, slow, though the language she hears is not her own.

4 | *Giga, in Victoria, your final days*

I can't keep up. My pulse races in the offices where we learn how quickly a life comes to its end. I hold your hand. Notes on a clipboard, blood pressure, the number of tumours gathered in a body. You refuse the treatments, remembering the needle through your chest wall, the first discovery of the malignant pleural effusion.

How quickly the years passed, how quickly we grew apart, too late the return, the counterpoint of our footwork, you holding my arm as we walked to the X-ray room, my boots brisk on the polished floor. Your chest on the screen, the technician comes to me, says how sorry she is, how sorry. She takes my hands in hers and then I slip away, unpartnered. You are in the changing room, unable to lift your arms to put on your camisole, your scar uncovered, a vine of stitches like brambles covering where your breast had been, notes, notes on a long line, nicked with rests, yours, mine, how quickly the years do pass.

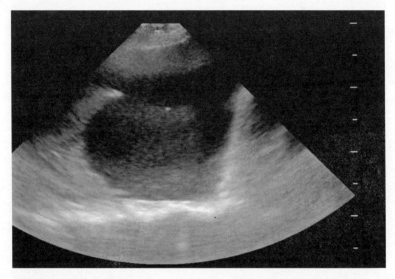

Ultrasound of a pleural effusion. [Adapted from Cotton, D.W., Lenz, R., Kerr, B. & Ma, I. (2018). "Point of Care Ultrasound for the General Internist: Pleural Effusions." Canadian Journal of General Internal Medicine, *13(2), p. 26.]*

5 | *Ciaccona, first thing in the morning, a walk to Chesterman Beach*

Move forward, linger, pause, advance the notes so perfectly timed, a bow of carbon, ebony, ivory, mother of pearl, abalone, bone, silk for the grip, advance, oh bow, lingering.

There are passages that find old sore places in my heart and remind them of the impact, the moment before the bruise. Yet how can that be? Notes, notes: inked marks on a five-line staff, one after another. A time signature. All of it an approximation, a correspondence, a calling to the page what is heard in the mind. I imagine his fingers playing the air, dipping a quill into ink, iron gall ink darkening to purple-black, a bruise in the quick ovals of the notes, the iron of it oxidizing on the paper and turning the notes brown. As a body turns to grey ash in the flame of cremation.

When the phone rang in the small hours and a nurse told me my mother had died, I felt punched, slammed in the chest, and I had to sit down on the carpet with the phone in my hand. I'd only tracked her down the evening before, a Sunday, and learned from a nurse that she'd been admitted to hospital the day before (we'd seen her the day before *that*) and wasn't expected to last the night. She danced toward me on a long beach.

A heart's anatomy: four chambers, two atria, right and left; two ventricles, left and right; and the wall that separates them. (Step, step.) Her heart weakened as her lungs worked harder to pass the oxygenated blood back, harder as she gasped, found it difficult to manage the oxygen tank she never wanted, the rhythm fading, fading, one, two, gasp, her eyes fluttering. The wall that separated us, the dance slowing, slowing, the two-part pumping losing a rhythm she'd known all her (my) life. That I knew in utero and must find now.

It is the counterpoint of the self, the pulse that guides us through our days, left, right, the rhythm strong, then fading, the composer arriving home to learn that his beloved wife had died, was buried. "On one stave, for a small instrument, the man writes a whole world of the deepest thoughts and most powerful feelings."[6] His sorrow ours for the time it takes to draw notes out of sixty-four bars, twenty-nine variations on four strings, taking us to the end of time. Pernambuco, abalone, ivory, bone. As my grandmother walked, slow, with her children, one a baby wrapped in a shawl, in the snow on the road away from the village forever.

Or, first thing in the morning, a walk to Chesterman Beach which was almost empty, except for a few early risers with their joyous dogs. Mist, two huge ravens muttering and poking in the flotsam. *I'd been thinking a great deal about geographical loneliness.*

The others arrive. We are a family of twenty-nine, we gather later on the beach, gather as I remove my parents' ashes from the bags within boxes and mix a scoop of each into Ziploc bags for those who want to take a portion to other places—a grove of trees, a hill, the corner of a room. Then a scoop of each, cinders and bone fragments, into an ice cream bucket for each family—mine, my brothers'—to take down the beach as a group and say what they need to say.

There are seven in my own group. We go to the water's edge and I tell my parents I loved them. I love them now, in the eyes and

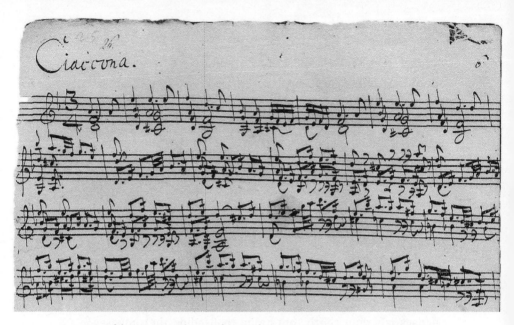

*Opening of the ciaccona or chaconne from Bach's 1720 manuscript. [Chaconne, Partita No.
2 in D minor, BWV 1004 (Bach, Johann Sebastian), 1720. International Music Score Library Project
(IMSLP), https://imslp.org/wiki/Violin_Partita_No.2_in_D_minor%2C_BWV_1004_(Bach%2C_
Johann_Sebastian)]*

legs and hands of my children, from them, from each, (my own
cheekbones), and wish them peace. I bend down and let the waves
wash into the bucket and out, two times, three times, as we all cried,
watching what remained of them join the water, some of their bone
fragments sinking into the wet sand, shining as mica shines, as the
waves retreated, to be taken by crabs or clams or a rough-throated
raven. And we retreated, back along the track we had made to the
water, in slow time, a long harmonic progression, some of us holding
hands, arms around my shoulders as I cried, slow, slow, the bass
line underlying all the voices, our voices, entwined, each with a
different version of their story, stories, triple time, slowed to the beat
a heart makes from birth to death, expanding, contracting more than
3.5 billion times, as these tides rise and fall, 122,640 times, a life
expanding and contracting, rising and falling, and we are flotsam on
this long beach. We are the sweet notes of the violin, fingers stopping,
finding the sorrow in the gut strings, the metal wound strings, steel,
aluminum, gold; we are the string to their bow, hair from the tails

of Siberian, Polish, Mongolian horses, raised in cold climates, and strong. Black hairs more grabby, pale hairs more silken. Slow, the stroking of hairs across strings, my mother's hand on my head in sickness, in distress. My hand on her head that final day, sparse hair springy under my palm.

We are still here, though the warheads have been mentioned, the fury of retaliation. Though hurricanes whirl across the planet, rivers flood, and wildfires burn entire towns. On a long beach I have put my mother and father into the tide. I am still here, though plastics fill our oceans and rivers break their dams. A violin, the last bars. Slow, slow, the return to a fire, the embrace of those who remain.

Blue Portugal

That journey is far,
where your love rests...[1]

1|

The first time we drank Modrý Portugal was in a restaurant in
Prague, near the State Opera House on Wilsonova where we had
tickets for *Aida* later on that evening. We'd noticed the restaurant on
our way to the opera house the morning we walked over to buy tickets.
(The older we get, the more reluctant we are to leave anything to
chance: hotels, dinners, tickets to the opera.) It looked Czech. By that
I mean it wasn't gussied up as a pizza place or hung with red paper
lanterns to advertise its Chinese specialties. The menu in the window
promised duck and pork and various dumplings, things we'd later
learn to enjoy—the large portions, the dense sauces—though at that
time, we were so new to the country that we had yet to eat things we
could definitely call "Czech." The menu also promised braised red
cabbage, which a Polish couple we met in in Brno swore was not
Czech at all but Polish! (Yet I do remember the huge red cabbages in
Zelný trh, the bins of caraway seed, and bushels of apples ready to
slice thinly to braise with the vegetables.) This was our first visit

to the Czech Republic and we were ready to plunge into its culture, its history, and its cuisine. We didn't realize how porous a border could be.

What wine would you recommend, we asked the waiter, who was friendly, using American idioms in his greeting (How you guys doing? Take a load off, my friend.) which fooled us into thinking his English was better than it was. Wine, he answered (or echoed), and brought us a bottle of Modrý Portugal, pouring it with a flourish as we ordered our meal. The delicious česnečka for me—garlic broth, soft potato, with cubes of fried bread and grated cheese. John ordered chicken livers with almonds and was surprised to be presented with a plate of prawns. The waiter's obvious pride in the dish and our growing suspicion that his English was illusory (as indeed was our Czech, and we were in his city after all) stopped John from making any fuss, though we were so far from any ocean, and the prawns had a tired whiff of old salt. Then a wonderful Hovězí guláš, which reminded me of an aunt's recipe passed along to my mother, one I always assumed was Hungarian, from my uncle's side of the family, not realizing that it probably came from my grandmother. (Those porous borders, that history.) The guláš was served with houskový knedlik, bread dumplings that soaked up the copious gravy.

And the wine? Beautiful. Ruby-coloured, light, not acidic or heavy with tannins. It was perfect with the food. Later, in Brno, we were told that "modrý" means blue. And Portugal, I asked? Well, just Portugal. (There's a story that an Austrian brought the grape from Oporto to his estate near Vienna in the late eighteenth century but ampelographers, who use leaf and berry shape as well as genetic fingerprinting to pinpoint the identity and origins of vines, dispute this provenance.)

I think now of the difficulties in my search for my own origins— the pruned shoots of my mother's family tree, the tangled roots of my father's, with grafts and sports on every limb. And drinking a wine like Blue Portugal seems the perfect accompaniment to both the search and the failure.

2|

The path to my mother's house is grown over with weedy clover.

Growing up, I knew nothing about my paternal grandmother's origins, apart from the name of the village she came from. My father repeated it as a kind of chant, but would go no further with information. She could speak Polish so I thought, well, Poland. But her country wasn't Poland, though it turns out her village is near the borders of both Poland and Slovakia. Her citizenship was Czech. The language she spoke wasn't even Polish but a dialect: Cieszyn Silesian, a hybrid spoken language, with feet in Poland, Slovakia, and the Czech lands of Bohemia, Moravia, and Czech Silesia.

Horni Lomná, the village where she was born, is small; its current population is less than 400. Friends drove us there in late February, the second time we travelled to the Czech Republic. In snow, it was beautiful, the low houses along the frozen river, the spruce trees hung with icicles, and everywhere the smell of smoke, as dark and earthy as peat. What wood produces that smoke, I wondered, or was it coal? That would make sense—turf or peat being a primitive form of coal, earth with a high carbon content. The scent accompanied us as we walked the slippery road to find her house, its number, 26, on a post by a little lane leading over a bridge and past a log house built closer to the road.

My grandmother grew up in that small village. She was Anna Klusova, daughter of Adam Klus and Eva Szkanderova. There are other names, a long line of them running across paper like the blue thread of the Lomná River I see on the map in front of me. Number 26, Horni Lomná, just near the river, a small bridge crossing it by the road, and then a path, deep with snow in late February of 2012. I could see her house from the cleared yard of the house directly in front of hers but I couldn't cross the white field to peer in the windows where she must have looked through to see what was going on in the world of sheep and spruce trees. Deer pausing to drink from the river, or maybe a fugitive wolf, or a goshawk swooping down to take up a shrew in its talons. I know these animals exist today in the Mionsi forest above the house and in those years their numbers must have been considerable. In fairy tales, the young girl walking home alone was often shadowed by a wolf. The church where my grandmother worshipped and was married is perhaps a mile from her house, a spring-fed well of cold holy water by the stairs to the narthex. I imagine her walking home from Mass with her scarf pulled up over her face against the wind and hearing wolves in the mountains, knowing they would enter her sleep in the bed she surely shared with a sister or two. She noted the stamp of lynx paws in the snow as they led over the bridge and up into the trees.

The windows where she looked through: I've seen them. Or I thought I saw them. A couple of years later I find out that the house was demolished during the decade of my birth and another, almost identical, was built in its place. Same number, same plain wooden structure, in the vernacular style I saw throughout the Czech Republic and Slovakia, some of them huddled in fields as the train passed. In Rožnov pod Radhoštěm, a whole village of these houses, preserved as a museum, and the new house could have joined that village as easily as anything, set into place in their clearing, near a wooden church that smelled of ancient forests. A chimney, so they had a fireplace, and of course they would have baked bread, something that I always consider when I think of large families and the necessity of filling their stomachs. My father didn't cook much but he did make pancakes and he always put buckwheat flour in them. Buckwheat figures in some of the dishes of the Beskydy Mountains so perhaps my grandmother's father, described in my grandmother's certificate of birth and baptism as a farmer, well, perhaps he grew buckwheat on that slope of hill behind the house. Maybe oats or tall rye. There were fruit trees under a burden of snow. Plums? Apples? In summer photographs, the valley of the Lomná River is verdant and lush. I imagine the taste of apples grown there, fed by those waters, plum brandy in clouded bottles.

On the meadow, meadow green,
near the well's stone rim…

Can a relationship be recreated with such modest ingredients?
With the possibility of buckwheat, the dream of wolves as my grandmother walked home from church? Only think of bread—pulverized
wheat berries, rye meal, water, yeast. Salt had to be brought into the
area for sheep and for people; they traded plum jam, slivovice, woollen
goods, and cheese. In that small house, its windows with their doubled
view of her time, of my time, I imagine the bowl of dough rising by the
hearth, curds in a wooden trough, and jars of plums gleaming on
a shelf.

And cabbage, that staple. Potatoes in many forms—as stryky, or
another kind of pancake, cooked on a blacha without oil and served
with cream or butter and some kind of pork, bacon, or crackling.

On a winter evening, candles flickering, the sound of wolves would
have brought to mind a folk song, a fairy story. Her story. My own.

3|

Trummer (1841) mentioned the existence of very old
"Blauer Portugieser" vines in Lower Styria in vineyards
and gardens, which was confirmed by Dietl in 1850.[2]

4|

I ate česnečka in Prague, in the restaurant before the opera, in the
taverna on Stepanska where I ate one bowl, then another (because I
couldn't imagine anything tasting so good at that moment). In Rožnov,
at Avion, surrounded by new leaves, in the Green Cat in Brno on the
first night of a return visit, accompanied not by Modrý Portugal but by
a light Veltlínské Zelené, tiny bubbles making their way up the glass.

Postcard of the Lomná River, 1913, the year my grandmother left her childhood home.

5 |

I grew up here in an open field...

This is my grandmother's village in the Czech Republic in 1913, the year she left for Canada. She was born in a house on a road along the Lomná River, *this* river. Recently, John and I were gifted with tickets to a wonderful recital by the young Hungarian pianist Zoltán Fejérvári, a beautiful programme of Schumann, Bartók, and Janáček. The short encore was one of the pieces from the Janáček cycle, *On an Overgrown Path*. It made me cry. I thought I was hearing something close to my family story and in a way I was. Janáček was born in Hukvaldy, not very far from my grandmother's village. *On an Overgrown Path* is based on Moravian folk songs and the title comes from one song with that opening line. It's a bride's song: a young woman remembering her life before marriage. I'm listening to the cycle now, played beautifully by Radoslav Kvapil. I'm hearing my grandmother's story, her memories of her mother's house, the anguish she must have felt at the deaths of two children (two pieces allude to the death of Janáček's daughter Olga), the sound of the little night owl in the Mionší forest. I wonder if she passed this part of the river as she left Horni Lomná forever with her five children, on her way to Antwerp, then Saint John, and eventually Drumheller where her husband was waiting. When I look at the house that replaced her mother's house, I imagine the earlier shelter in her dreams, as it is in mine. The windows might even be the same windows, sanded and repaired and used again.

Where does the sweet apple's path end
there shall the maid find her young man.

6|

It is very probable that the cradle of "Blauer Portugieser" and "Blaufränkisch" is Lower Styria.[3]

The borders always shifting, archduchies and principalities, entire countries absorbed and then eventually released. Slovenia, Austria, the Kingdom of Serbs, Croats, Slovenes, Burgenland, Illyria. And certainly wine would have been served, made from those ancient vines that never saw Portugal, never waited out an Iberian winter for spring and the wild irises at Sagres, the oranges and lemons bright on their branches in February, near Faro, the cool-tiled churches. Perhaps a name gives a plant notions, that it could travel in winters to settle by the sea in a canvas lounge chair, sip a little wine itself (a dry vinho verde, a rich port), could stow away in a corner of a vessel heading to South Africa or the New World. To overhear a woman praying with her children in the great loneliness of steerage quarters, rough linen valise under the bunk, diapers drying on an improvised line.

7|

I have already crossed three mountains and woods...

I have the passenger list for the *Mount Temple* sailing which brought my grandmother to Saint John, New Brunswick from Antwerp,

The small farm where my grandmother grew up.

Belgium in 1913. The *Mount Temple* carried 485 passengers, of whom 477 travelled in steerage. Eight passengers had cabins.

In truth, I've had the passenger list for a couple of years and it was only today that I realized I'd had an entirely erroneous notion of her voyage. I saw that she was listed as "wife" and that five other names were included, one of them Josef, which was the name of her first husband, Josef Yopek. But it wasn't until just now that I read more carefully (or at least understood the handwriting more clearly) and saw that the other five names were all listed as "children" so that the Josef must have been her son, Joe, later known to my brothers and me as Uncle Joe. She was travelling with five children: Paul and John, a set of twins, aged no more than four, Joseph who would have been three, Barbara, two, and Frank, perhaps a year old. Investigating further, I discover her husband came to Canada more than a year earlier. She was joining him, bringing a child he almost certainly hadn't yet seen.

A report on steerage conditions for the period that my grandmother voyaged from Europe to North America says this:

> The sleeping quarters are large compartments, accommodating as many as 300, or more, persons each. For assignment to these, passengers are divided into three classes; namely, women without male escorts, men traveling alone, and families. Each class is housed in a separate compartment and the compartments are often in different parts of the vessel. It is generally possible to shut off all communication between them, though this is not always done.
>
> The berths are in two tiers, with an interval of 2 feet and 6 inches of space above each. They consist of an iron framework containing a mattress, a pillow, or more often a life-preserver as a substitute, and a blanket. The mattress, and the pillow if there is one, is filled with straw or seaweed.
>
> On some lines this is renewed every trip. Either colored gingham or coarse white canvas slips cover the mattress and pillow. A piece of iron piping placed at a height where it will separate the mattresses is the "partition" between berths. The blankets differ in weight, size, and material on the different lines.[4]

She was thirty-two years old. How did she travel from Horni Lomná to Antwerp, with five children under the age of six, including a set of twins? Herding them onto trains, each responsible for a valise, a cloth bag. There would have been diapers. A lullaby at bedtime, a story, a promise of their papa at the end of the journey. When I knew her, as a small child, I thought her English was cursory. At family gatherings she was quiet. I hear the clamour of human activity on that ship and I think of her with the children clinging to her skirt, sleeping on a bed of seaweed or straw, moving across water, into another language, a landscape so utterly foreign.

In Portugal, in 2015, more than fifty years after my grandmother's death, I gaze into a glass case of artefacts taken from shipwrecks at the National Museum of Archaeology's *Time Salvaged from the Sea* exhibit and read a card that talks of the sea voyage in terms I understand as deeply as I've ever understood anything. A ship is a society closed in on itself, it tells me. Yes, me. I am the only one in the room at that moment. I am leaning my face to the glass and reading, while time stops, takes me backwards.

> ...a ship represents an architectural structure that is destined to travel, equipped for the survival of her inhabitants who are isolated at sea for weeks or months on end.
>
> The internal distribution of this human microcosm, confined by wooden planks, iron, the clouds and saltwater, reflects, in its own particular way, the organization and hierarchy of a society on land that drove this community to its fate.
>
> During the crossing, for hundreds of men...women and children, stern and bow decks, poop deck, topsail or hold became opposite poles of a small world saturated with divisions between social classes and geographical loneliness.[5]

Among clouds and saltwater, between Antwerp and Saint John, my grandmother let go of her village, her family who'd lived there for generations, her language, her apprehension of seasons among spruce, beeches, and fields of tall grass, a river running by the lane to her house, the Lomná: "It was mentioned in 1592 as przi rzece Lomny."[6] The name is derived from the words łom (clatter, rumble, susurrus) or załom (turn, bend). Logs were floated down it to Jablunkov through the Mionsi forest. She left her country, that green forest, the snowy Beskydy Mountains, and after more than two weeks at sea, she became a foreigner. The small town she arrived at was saturated with divisions and I can only imagine her loneliness, geographical or otherwise. She was foreign for the rest of her life.

I think of her arriving in Saint John, in March (it would have been snowy) and trying to find her bearings in that new world. Perhaps Joseph Yopek met her and took her to Drumheller. But I suspect he didn't. Maybe she managed the train trip across the new country with ease, although she spoke no English. The *Mount Temple* manifest indicates she had 200 dollars, a large sum for that time. Maybe she was more worldly than I give her credit for (though credit is not the right word. I've seen her village tucked up against the flank of a mountain, heard the Lomná river running under ice, and that's world enough, the deep shade of spruce trees on summer days, the snow in winter muffling all sound; she needs no credit from me) but what if she wasn't?

Somehow she found her way to her husband in Alberta. They'd been separated at least a year. Their second daughter Marion was born nine and a half months later, in Drumheller.

8 |

Vine-writing (ἄμπελος "vine" + γραφή "writing")

Like so many others, I sent a sample of my saliva to a company that promised to tell me who I am. It took a month. The results weren't surprising though of course I hoped for something more specific: 44% Eastern Europe and Russia, 18% Ireland/Scotland/Wales, 17% Great Britain, 6% France, 6% Germanic Europe, 6% Sweden, 3% Baltic States. I hoped I'd be taken to a valley, to a plot of earth, shown an ancient tree, and told this is you. I wanted to know who contributed what. All the riddles of quantity, genesis, answers neatly presented on a map of the world.

In ampelography, individual grape cultivars can be distinguished from one another by the analysis of nuclear DNA microsatellites. It's a complicated science and I don't pretend to understand it very well, but the process has offered researchers huge surprises. For example, the popular Chardonnay grape of Burgundy was almost certainly the result of an accidental cross between the Pinot grape of that region and an inferior variety, Gouais blanc, which has been banned in wine production because it produces such poor-quality wine.

My surprises are French ancestors, Swedish forefathers or mothers, the Baltic farmers who might have bred with the Eastern Europeans.

Studies of modern plants projected back in time can be misleading. A wild plant may have grown over a larger or smaller area, or its seeds may have been dispersed and gained a foothold far from the parent plant's habitat. Climates change, forests are cleared, and sheep and goat grazing cause environmental deterioration. Ancient botanical remains provide a way around this problem, enabling the ancient landscape and biosphere to be reconstructed from direct, contemporaneous evidence. They also provide an absolute time scale for genetic change.

How far away was the home of the man who married her first, before my grandfather, the man with the Polish name and the brother in Canada? The one who went ahead to make a home for them, the home I grew up thinking was a homestead taken out under the Dominion Lands Act but which was, instead, a shack in a squatters' community on the Red Deer River? Yes, there was a brother-in-law, who disappeared, and her own brother, arriving a few months after her, who lived in a dwelling dug into the side of a hill.

> *There's one hasn't made it,*
> *and he was a friend of mine.*
> *He lies there on the hillside...*

9|

> *Our house has a garden at the front...*

It has fruit trees, a hollow that could be a creek, a fence to keep animals close to the house. A pig? Some sheep? Perhaps a cow. My grandmother learned to make cheese before she came to Canada, fresh curds my father loved; she made butter to sell, and noodles golden with eggs from the chickens that ranged through the yard of the house in Drumheller, even entering the house for crumbs or the cool shade of midday in summers. Did she ever sing the songs I am listening to now, the folk poetry of her area, did she hum as she made cheese, did she dream of a true love coming from the mountains as she washed clothes in a big tub behind the house, within the sound of the Lomná River?

> *The river will flow away,*
> *and nor is love here to stay,*
> *it too will pass forever,*
> *like a rosemary leaf it will wither.*

10 |

Everything that came along: people, birds, bees, gnats; humming of wind, clap of thunder; swirling of a waterfall, buzz of hundreds of years old trees and whispering of a leaf, when it fell on cold soil in the autumn.[7]

11 |

From my journal, June 29, 2013

The dream was as natural as life. She was there, sitting in a big chair, and I sat with her, my daughter (about fifteen) at my other side. I held her hands with their long cool fingers. She had almost no accent. If the dream had been real life, she'd have been about 120.

We talked. I can't really remember what we talked about but I was sorry I'd left it so long. I didn't say this to her but I felt it intensely: if I'd known she was still alive, I'd have visited much sooner.

Holding her hand, I turned my face close to hers. I went to Horni Lomná, I told her, and tears ran down her cheeks. I should have brought you a picture. But those trees...

She said, not as an interruption, but as a memory: there were plum trees, and apples. The tears coursed their way down her wrinkled cheeks, water finding a route across dry land.

And spruce? I asked. Spruce, on the road leading to the church? She nodded.

And is it the Lomná River that passes just in front of the house, with the little bridge over it?

She didn't say anything.

I put my daughter's hand in hers. This is your great-grand-daughter, I said. But she was thinking about something else, her thin hair pulled into a bun and her house-dress faded. Or perhaps she couldn't see us there in the room where none of the dates fit together—her birth, the trees covered with snow in February in Horni Lomná, the age she was when I was born, my own age when she died, and what would a woman dead for five decades be thinking about in a room with two strangers sitting beside her? Maybe the plum trees by that small house, maybe the weather, maybe the years and what they'd brought, and taken.

12 |

The knowledge about grapevine cultivars progenitors discloses the genetic composition and geographical origin of cultivars, assists to trace back migration routes and to estimate their distribution and importance in former times.[8]

13 |

This here is the narrow path
as winds through the vineyards
that I would tread along…

Listening to the young pianist[9] playing Janáček's "In the Mists," I close my eyes and imagine the landscape where you were born. Foothills of the Beskydys, near Janáček's home village.

He was a folklorist as well as a musician and gathered the songs and spoken tales of Moravia-Silesia. Did you sing? Did your family have its own musicians? Did you listen to the bells on the sheep and imagine them into simple tunes? Listening, I am in Moravia, I am in a village of white buildings painted with ultramarine flowers by Anežka Kašpárková,[10] I am myself a babička, stitching blue cloth in long red stitches, my four grandchildren running in the tall grass.

Listening to the young pianist playing "In the Mists," I hear birdsong, the brittle canes of winter roses brushing against my house, the sounds you would not have noticed in your daily work (a house without roses), feeding chickens, washing the laundry of a family of ten, then nine, then eight, then rising again, the deaths and births echoing the seasons, the river freezing, thawing, the return of green leaves on the cottonwoods in Drumheller, on the beeches of your childhood home in Moravia-Silesia, all of it hidden in mist, morning mist coming down off the Beskydy Mountains, frozen mist in your final years in Beverly, a stone's throw from the North Saskatchewan River.

Listening to the young pianist playing "The Madonna of Frydek," I am in the fields of barley, soft grasses, poppies. A blown-away leaf, the composer said, could be heard as a love song.[11] The children are running ahead, a bag of apples slung over the back of the oldest.

Listening to the young pianist playing "The Madonna of Frydek," I remember the sign for Frydek as we drove to your village. We drove on, past the sign, past the coat of arms for Horni Lomná, drove on, through snow, past the church with the spring of eternal waters (said to have cured those suffering cholera), past the graveyard inaccessible in snow, the miracles of Mary, and a road ghosted by the footsteps of my grandmother's family, her two sisters, the brother whom no one remembers, who died in his dugout house in a squatters' camp in Drumheller during another epidemic, hearing them somehow in the snow, the light wind, and now in the penultimate chord as the pianist completes his encore. Now, now, now. I am applauding and I am brushing tears from my eyes in the dark hall.

14 |

Where we drank Modrý Portugal

In Prague, with pizza. In Olumouc, after a reading at Palacký University's Konvict, when we invited the entire audience to join us at the bar for a drink. In Ostrava. ("On its own it can be also a good companion."[12]) In Bratislava. In the lovely Exil bookstore and wine bar in Prague again, at a reading organized by the Canadian Embassy, and where (again) we ordered wine for the small-ish audience who'd come to hear us read our work in English and then in Czech by young students who'd translated selected pieces. At Falk Café in Brno, across from Masaryk University where we taught a week-long course in Canadian literature and around the corner from that, another café whose name escapes me but where we had delicious open-faced sandwiches late afternoon with colleagues, accompanied by glasses of cool Blue Portugal or Veltlínské Zelené and where a small fire burned (Michael wore a red scarf wrapped twice around his neck). At Špalíček, our last night in the Czech Republic, with česnečka and roast duck. From my window I could see the statue of Mozart in front of Reduta, commemorating his concert there at the age of eleven, with his older sister Nannerl, in 1767. One wing sprouts from his naked shoulder. I sipped my wine and wondered, again, why I was leaving this country. Sometimes I tasted flowers, though it was winter. Sometimes, smoke. I thought of the peaty smoke as we walked away from my grandmother's house, the house I thought was hers without knowing, then, that it had fallen and another rose in its place, how I could smell it in my jacket for days, new world wool reacquainted with old world sheep, and the smoke from all the chimneys in the village.

How Rivers Break Away
and Meet Again

Let me then, like a child advancing with bare feet into a cold river,
descend again into that stream.
—VIRGINIA WOOLF[1]

Prologue

I am a reader of atlases. I've always been drawn to them. Looking into
the tattered cloth-bound copies in the classrooms of my childhood,
I could dream my way onto continents so far away it was tomorrow
there as I traced borders with a wondering finger. I remember learning
how to use the legend, that the little box with lines and colour charts
provided visual aids to help you to understand where land rose above
sea level, how deep the sea was, how some cities were larger than
others by the circle used to represent them. Was it infilled, was it red,
did it contain a star? There were the principal roads and the other
roads, thin lines (usually red), going from one circle or dot to another,
across borders, through the shadings that meant mountains. And the
thin blue lines, scribbling across the map, widening to pools, meeting
other rivers, breaking away again, finally reaching one ocean or
another. It never occurred to me, as a child allowed to borrow an atlas

during a wet recess or because I'd finished my assignments early, that someone might actually *own* an atlas, or several, that the pages would show how borders shift, how rivers change, oxbow, leave their banks, join with other watercourses, enter lakes, the waters amalgamating. Yet somehow a river can leave again, return to its original course, sure of its water.

I have the Oxford *New Concise World Atlas*, third edition, and lately I've been keeping it on the low table by our woodstove, lifting it to my lap in quiet moments to check the routes of rivers. Specific rivers, the ones I've travelled along or walked across on bridges. In Ostrava a young man took me for a glass of wine (it was beautiful golden Pálava) and as we sat in the little bar, he pointed out the window to a bridge at the end of the street, spanning the Ostravice River. If you cross that bridge, you are in Silesia, he said, smiling. (I've been trying to figure out what he meant ever since.)

And on the low table, books about human anatomy, atlases of the strange geography of our bodies, with their own legends. It's the veins I'm particularly interested in. They are usually indicated in blue, as opposed to arteries, which are red to represent the oxygen-rich blood carried away from the heart to the rest of the body. The blood the veins return to the heart is darker, because it is oxygen-depleted. In one of the veins of my leg, a clot formed, though there's no sign of it now.

I find the rivers I love, the ones I dream about. I find them in the atlas and realize they too have their difficulties. They rise in springs or seep from marshes or the melting of glaciers, they gather, they flow, so clean in their beginnings, and unless they become grounded or are endorheic, they arrive at the great oceans of the world full of the silts, the effluents, the timbers and old cars and snowmelt and rain of their journeys. There will have been diversions. There will have been accidents. There might have been meanders and braidings and temporary islands and dams.

A deep river, two or three houses in bamboo quiet,
And such goings on: red blossoms glaring with white![2]

1 | *Iliac vein, femoral vein, popliteal vein, tibial vein, greater saphenous vein, lesser saphenous vein*

A deep cramping pain. Some swelling. In the emergency room, my history is taken: pulmonary embolism a year ago; suspected deep vein thrombosis; suspected metastases in both lungs (though they've disappeared); six months of blood thinners; and many scans and tests.

A lab technician is called from his bed to take my blood for a D-dimer test to determine if there is active clot activity. An ultrasound is set for the next morning, though it is well into that morning when the technician draws blood from a pool of my right arm. I do not wait for the results because I want some sleep and the person in the other bed is on a powerful narcotic that makes her itchy, causes her to moan on her side of the screen that separates us. The medical staff is not happy I'm leaving.

We drive home on a dark highway. It's a forty-five-minute journey and after thirty minutes the emergency room physician phones me on my husband's cell phone. In the car, the loud opening chords of "Sultans of Swing," a moment when I regret he didn't set his ring tone to something sweet—Brahms' "Lullaby" or "That Sheep May Safely Graze"—as I stab at the screen to answer the call. "Hello, hello?" The physician tells me that my D-dimer test is positive for blood clotting, that I may have a DVT, and that I must return immediately to begin a course of anticoagulants.

"As I'll be coming in later in the morning for an ultrasound, I can't just wait until then?"

"No, I must insist you come back now."

So we turn around and head back, my husband silent with weariness. He won't let me drive. He's more than a little irritated that I insisted we leave before the test results were ready. We don't talk, but then about halfway to the hospital, at Middlepoint, we see a large animal on the side of the highway. Not an elk, which often pause on the road-sides before crossing and we always joke that if you see one, there are ten more in the bushes behind it. And not a coyote. Bigger than that. It takes a moment or two, and the glare of the animal's golden eyes, for us to realize we're seeing a cougar. I've lived on this peninsula for thirty-five years and I've seen just two cougars in that time. I've heard two more, I think, but sightings are rare. We are both excited and forget for a moment where we are going, and for what.

All down the coast, we pass creeks in the darkness, Homesite, Meyer, Anderson, Maple, Haskins, scribbling down the mountains. And I would do it all again, sit at the desk with a nurse taking my pulse, my blood pressure, arranging for bloodwork, ultrasound, medication to prevent a blood clot moving up into my lungs, for the glow of the cougar's eyes in our headlights, and the knowledge of water finding its way to the sea.

An eleven-mile tributary of the Olza River, flowing through the small village where my grandmother was born, a corner of what's now the Czech Republic, not far from the Slovak border, where the river originates. The name has its origins in clatter, susurrus, or bend, noting the sound it makes over stones under spruces and black poplars, and perhaps from the storks who lend their name to a nearby village the river passes on its way to the Olza. When I walked along the river, it was winter and everything was frozen but I paused on the bridge that led to my grandmother's house and imagined its waters, its sound, dreaming of it later as she must have remembered it, in Drumheller, scattering scraps for the hens and clapping her hands to scare away the coyotes who waited for their moment.

3 | *Englishman River*

As a child, I camped there with my family. It wasn't a swimming river, at least not where the provincial campsite was located, by the falls, which tumbled fast and white into bottle-green pools I watched for ages from a bridge over a narrow point. I was high, high, but I could feel the cool spray on my face. At night there was a game with other kids in the campsite, a tracking game, where one team had a head-start and left a trail of arrows made with sticks or else long stems of grass twisted onto salal. I remember hiding in what seemed like a cave but was the hollow created by the roots of an enormous fallen tree. I crouched and waited, hearing the voices of the other kids in the falling light.

We never visited the estuary in those years but later I walked with a friend and saw mew gulls, Thayer's gulls, glaucous-winged gulls, common murres, black oystercatchers, hundreds of Black Brant geese, Canada geese, widgeon, and mallards, buffleheads, and goldeneye.

When I was a young woman sad enough to consider ending my life, I stood on the bridge in November. I was driving by myself to Long Beach after a series of humiliating events during the first term of my fourth year at the University of Victoria; I had permission to take a week away from classes. I'd borrowed my father's red Datsun pickup truck. It had a canopy, which leaked, and a canvas hammock, sewn by my father with his big careful stitches, strung diagonally across the bed of the truck. I rigged up a plastic bag over the vent in the ceiling of the canopy to catch the drips and smoothed my sleeping bag into the narrow hammock and walked out to the bridge. I had my family's dog with me, a crazy Samoyed–Lab cross. He bit people if he was allowed off his leash but he liked me and he was warm. He strained at his leash on the bridge and I thought about jumping off into the deep green water. I didn't want to think about what would happen to my body but I also couldn't imagine what would happen to the dog on his leash if I died at Englishman River where no one knew I'd gone and wouldn't think to look for me. The dog was my wavering. I also wanted to give him the gift of wild running on the empty beaches I knew we'd find that time of year. We returned in the rain to the truck and I heated soup for myself on the little blue Optimus stove and scooped some Gravy Train into the dog's bowl. I ate my soup on the tailgate in my rain jacket while the dog huddled under the picnic table. Then we both made ourselves as comfortable as we could in the damp canopy and slept while the rain pounded on the roof, near enough to touch.

(A woman, hand inside her rain jacket, tenderly taking her pulse, the drama of her heart pushing blood, whoosh, into her circulatory system, the drama of her life, whoosh, at wrist, at neck. She wonders if she will move forward to the other side of the river, or back, into the wreckage of the past weeks while her dog pants at her feet, eager for more walking. Not this, not the dark considerations of life or death.)

Does a river remember in any way the small and large dramas enacted on the bridges spanning it? On the paths beside it, where a cougar might chase down a deer? In the water itself where the bodies of young people have been crushed when they tried to dive straight into the pools in summer? Does a river remember the children moving quietly near its banks at dusk, hiding in the huge root systems of tumbled cedars, arms wrapped around their knees, their parents calling in the space between campfires? Water never stopped falling from the rocks. Trees grew in their great age, then also fell, and huckleberry sprouted from their trunks.

If a woman looked down into water to find out where she belonged, if she saw anything of herself in the green pools, does anything remain?

4 | *The Fraser River at its origins high on the Continental Divide*

> A dripping spring just west of a pond at Fraser Pass is the
> source of British Columbia's longest river.[3]

We stopped at a Point of Interest on the Yellowhead Highway near
Mount Robson and walked along a rough trail to see the river, newly
tumbled down from its origins. The colour of the water was almost
tropical, greeny-blue, not the sludgy brown of the river as it courses
down through the Fraser Valley, dense with sediments and effluents from every industry along its banks. Dense in season with the
bodies of fish swimming strongly towards their own origins. Dense
with the drowned, the damaged, the fallen-from-cliffs, the hopeless.
Trees washed away in spring run-off, a fence post, a canoe pulled from
its mooring. "Proceeding up the River at length we had the pleasure
of camping on ground clear of snow, but the Mountains have all the
appearance of winter..."[4]

But at the lookout, it was aqua, it was light over rocks, it was
fresh. Further downstream, we saw rafts in white rapids, notices for
helicopter tours of the source. It was not yet far enough west for the
point where Simon Fraser began his exploration of what he believed
to be the Columbia River, leaving Fort George on May 28, 1808. We
were driving east, over the Divide, where the rivers changed direction.
And we stopped. Walked along a rocky trail to look into aqua-green
water, wondering how long a stick dropped into it would last on the
river's long journey to the Pacific Ocean.

5 | Breakup: Mackenzie River, Deh Cho (Dene), Kuukpak
(Inuvialuktun), Nagwichoonjik (Gwich'in), the River of
Disappointment (named this by Alexander Mackenzie, upon
reaching the Arctic and not the Pacific as he paddled
its great length)

We were in Fort Simpson in April and the Mackenzie River
looked to be still frozen though breakup was in the air. We could hear
the ice rumbling in both the Mackenzie and its major tributary the
Liard as the water began to find its way north beneath the ice. (Fort
Simpson is at the confluence of the two rivers.) Our host took us
for a historical tour of the village, pointing out where the York Boat
excavation had taken place, where the Pope had sermonized, the
squared-log McPherson house, which he explained was undergoing
restoration. And everywhere, there were trucks, the same trucks,
mud-covered and slowly cruising, windows open though it was
hardly warm, arms hanging out, flannel sleeves rolled up. Breakup
makes people restless, our host explained. All winter they can cross
on the ice-bridge and in summer there's a ferry across the river (Fort
Simpson is on an island), but at breakup, we're stranded! (We didn't
panic because we'd flown in and knew we were flying out again the
next day.) There was soft wind, the deep mud everywhere, grass
and aspens beginning to green. I thought of my father, working for a
time on one of the last Mackenzie River steamships, as a deckhand,
and I think he cut cordwood too. He was sixteen years old. Would
it have been the s s *Distributor*? The s s *Mackenzie*? I don't know,
though my son thinks it was the *Distributor*, which began its life on
the Thompson River. Both were decommissioned shortly after the
Second World War; my father had enlisted in the last years of the
war, then left the military to work in a meat-packing plant. It didn't
last and he enlisted again in the navy, learning a trade and raising
a family. (A report by an occupational counsellor says, "He enjoyed
working in confined quarters aboard ship.") But sometimes his eyes
would go dreamy and he'd remember the long hours of daylight on
the Mackenzie River and I wish now I'd asked about the work. (For so

many years, my heart was frozen in his company.) What kind of wood, how long it took to cut enough for the run, where he slept, what he ate, and if he ever thought of staying in that country. Did he remember the tundra swans, the snow geese, the sandhill cranes, moose in the shallows? I'm certain he fished. He fished in every river he ever knew. Did he remember the scent of spruce, of willows and wild roses, did he think ever of returning? When I showed him photographs, he was briefly interested and then dismissive. It's all changed now, he asserted. All changed.

6 | *Young lovers on the Seine*

You were thirty-one. I was twenty-four. We'd met, fallen in love, announced to the world we were marrying before the year ended. In Paris, we couldn't get along. Our room was too small, just a bed in a curve of the winding staircase of a hotel looking out on the Sorbonne, a bidet and sink under its window. There was nowhere to be alone and in each other's company we quarrelled. I told you I thought you were arrogant. You said I was a show-off, that my poetry was over the top. I hated the way you looked at the price of every meal on the chalkboard outside the restaurants. I wanted to get drunk and walk alone up the Montagne Sainte-Geneviève to the Pantheon. Instead, we booked a ride on a Seine boat, having watched the boats pass under any of the thirty-seven bridges we'd crossed on our daily perambulations, the Passerelle Debilly, Pont de l'Alma, Pont d'Arcole, Pont Saint-Louis, and decided it would be a good way to see the city from the slow-flowing river. The boat was enormous and every seat was filled. I barely remember what we saw because we decided, early on in the cruise, that we would break up as soon as we returned to Canada. Everything I looked at was through a haze of tears. This wasn't the way I wanted my life to go, arguing with someone who felt like a stranger on a river in the most beautiful city I'd ever slept in. I wanted to be held and kissed in narrow streets, wanted a glass of champagne at a tiny bar, a meal at a bistro with checked tablecloths and rough wine in tumblers. I didn't want to be quarrelling on the river or in the uncomfortable bed in the smelly hotel, the shared toilet behind the next door in the curving staircase. I remember you reached for my hand and it was as though the sun came out at that moment, though it didn't. As though the swans appeared only for us, though everyone leaned over the gunnels to take photographs of them swimming placidly under the Pont de la Tournelle.

7 | *Deep venous drainage system*

The fibular vein. Anterior tibial vein. Posterior tibial vein. The three become the popliteal vein at the knee; and then that vein enters the thigh, via a passageway called the adductor canal, as the femoral vein. These are the veins where the thrombosis formed, a clot poised like a temporary island, breaking free, travelling into my pulmonary system where it lodged as an embolism, threatening my heart.

My heart never knew it was threatened. My heart grew large with love that time, in anticipation of a third grandchild, surrounded by other family members, hearing their voices, sitting with them at the long table we'd eaten at for more than three decades. My heart, unaware, as I tried to catch my breath. It never knew it was threatened. It was filled with love, it was heavy with love. And other minor veins drain into the femoral vein, like small creeks. The femoral vein graciously receives its tributaries as rivers receive theirs, the threads of mountain courses, of run-off, of bog-dark sweet creekwater, limestone, gritty, clear as mirror glass, dense with salmon, lively with mayflies and dragonflies catching fire, of rivulets, right-bank, left-bank, forked, streamlet, greater saphenous vein, which usually receives the external pudendal vein as well as the superficial epigastric vein, and the superficial circumflex iliac vein.

When I go for my swim at the local pool, I see the older women whose aquatic fitness class is finishing just as I enter the water for my laps. They are thin, large, stooped, high-stepping, and lame. On their legs, the story of their lives thus far. Varicose veins, spider veins, venous insufficiency, superficial phlebitis, swellings and dark bruisings, lymphedema: some of them use walkers or canes to help them into and out of the water, to the hot-tub where they are helped down the stairs. But in the pool—sometimes I arrive early enough to see this—they raise their arms, they float, they are light as birds in the clear water while gentle music plays and the instructor leads their movements from the walkway at the edge. In the hot-tub after, their heads above the warm froth, they are beautiful, talking among themselves as the music continues and I swim my laps, listening to them.

...listen to your suppliant's voice, come, and benig-
nant in these rites rejoice; Give plenteous Seasons,
and sufficient wealth, and pour; in lasting streams,
continued Health.[5]

Once I told them, You look like goddesses, all of you, there in the water, so graceful as you raise your arms. Join us, one of them says, smiling, using her cane to walk unsteadily to the change room. My own legs are uncertain rivers, uncertain streams, their courses changing, islands forming of my own blood, its platelets and fibrins turned semi-solid.

8 | *The Rosebud River, between Home Coulee and the Red Deer River*

A Blackfoot word, *Akokiniskway*, meaning "the river of many roses."

Stop, I kept saying, stop. It was cold, we'd slept one night in the honeymoon suite at the Rosedeer Hotel in Wayne after an indifferent dinner in the atmospheric Last Chance Saloon. Our room was on the second floor. The third floor was apparently haunted, rooms where Ku Klux Klan thugs hired by the mines had beaten men identified as Communists. Burned them with cigarettes. Tarred them and feathered them and sometimes went too far. Our sleep was uninterrupted by the past. We'd risen, shivered our way to the cold car, and we left before 7:00 a.m., everything around us silent and crisp with frost, though we'd hiked in shirtsleeves the afternoon before above the townsite to look into old mine shafts, to lean down to prairie crocus, sunlight warm on our arms. Stop,

stop. Because the river had something to tell me. I couldn't quite hear. Something, something, about miners my grandfather might have known and hardship and what the fallen fence posts had kept contained. Magpies squabbled in the willows. The wild roses were not in leaf, not yet, but the bushes grew on the banks, promising faint perfume and a profusion of pink blossoms by June.

There was something that I knew as we stopped by the bridge. Air, the light falling over the hoodoos on Highway 10X. Magpies, whose ancestors may have shadowed my grandfather on his way to work, my aunts and uncles on their way to school, their lunch in lard pails. My thumb on the rusting blue of the bridge rasped a few syllables I'd never heard before, a whisper, You could live here. This road could be your route home. Stop.

9 | *Nicola River, named for Hwistesmexteqen, Walking Grizzly Bear, Chief N'kwala, its tributaries the Coldwater, the Spius, and Guichon Creek, the stretch between Spences Bridge and Merritt*

The first time, we were driving to a family gathering at Barriere and rather than drive Highway 1 up the canyon to Cache Creek, then east to Kamloops before heading north to our destination: we decided to take a slightly longer route, along Highway 8 to Merritt, then up Highway 5A to Kamloops. John knew this highway, though I couldn't remember my family ever driving it. Our road had always been Highway 1 or else the Crowsnest. We were almost always driving to Edmonton or further and my father wanted to get there quickly. But we meandered along Highway 8, along the most beautiful river I'd ever seen. It's the Nicola River, said John, and yes, we had the road map to prove it. It was a hot day. Our two children (at that time) were three and one. Our English sheepdog X was eleven, her coat thick and curly. The boys were restless in their car seats and we had picnic food so we stopped at a primitive forestry campsite for lunch. The ground was clear and open, tall Ponderosa pines provided dappled shade, the river was bright and clear, and our dog immediately plunged in to lie on her belly in the shallows. The boys made roads through pine needles for their little cars and trucks. There were rough tables of halved logs with stumps to sit on. Although the temperature must have been in the low 90s (this was pre-Celsius), the river's presence cooled us; its music was lovely as it raced over rocks, silvery, running half an octave, lightly, lightly. I remember drinking a cup of black coffee from a thermos and leaning my back against a warm stone rough with lichen. I was so grateful to my young husband for bringing me to this place. The low feathery tufts growing in the rubble near the river were somehow familiar to me. Southernwood? Was that the source of the fresh lemony smell? That, and the scent of pines, of tall sagebrush, of dry grass?

> ...for your love is better than wine,
> better than the fragrance of your perfumes.

Your name is a flowing perfume—
therefore young women love you.[6]

I imagined us staying there, making some sort of shelter to extend our small tent, I imagined a life by the river. My husband had his fishing rod, I knew a little about edible plants. Already I watched the sun for its own time.

...the beams of our house are cedars,
our rafters, cypresses.

We spread out our maps and planned the rest of the drive, eating sandwiches and apples, tipping our cup into the river itself (this was before anyone worried about giardia), drinking the cold water as sweet and satisfying as wine. There were outhouses and we used them, one of us staying with the boys as the other entered the little shed in order to at least have the opportunity for privacy and toilet paper (there'd been a stop or two along the way to crouch by the highway behind the door of the brown Toyota station wagon). John stretched out on the table for a short nap while I helped the boys to skip stones on the surface of the river. A small herd of mule deer were grazing on the opposite side, in a pasture under the shadow of the mountains the Nicola River cut through.

I adjure you, Daughters of Jerusalem,
by the gazelles and the does of the field,
Do not awaken or stir up love
until it is ready.

I changed diapers, rubbed sunscreen into the arms and legs of my children, the tops of their feet in leather Clarks (How beautiful are your feet in sandals...), and packed up our picnic leavings to return to the back of the car. We had several hours of travel ahead of us and as it turned out, a stop in Kamloops for an emergency car repair, so it was time to leave, though I've never forgotten the smell of the dry grass and sage, the sound of the water, and the arms of my small boys, golden and downy, as they tossed their stones as far as their arms could fling them before I settled them into the car.

Deep waters cannot quench love,
nor rivers sweep it away.

10 | *The superficial and deep veins of the sole*

Their beginnings at the dorsal arch of the foot, their commu-
nication with the digital veins between the toes, their confluences, the
multiple small tributaries, how they swell and ache, how the perfo-
rating veins connect the superficial veins with those in the deeper
compartments through canals dense with lymph nodes, how they
flow, flow, their fluids dark red, deoxygenated, en route to the lungs,
the great rivers sourced in our feet, unnoticed in their small beginnings until their braidings unravel, their banks collapse, islands break
free and impede the flow.

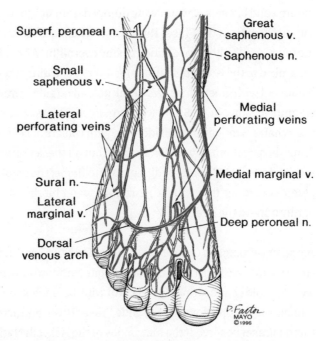

The venous system of the foot. [From Mozes G & Gloviczki P. Chapter 2, Venous Embryology
and Anatomy. In: Bergan JJ, editor. The Vein Book. New York: Elsevier, Inc., 2007, p.21; used with
permission of Mayo Foundation for Medical Education and Research, all rights reserved.]

11 | *The Fraser River, below Mile Zero Motel, Lillooet, BC*

> ...in the perpetual slide of mountain and forest, in the erosion of mountain and gumbo rangeland, in the impact of whirlpool and winter ice, the river is forever mad, ravenous and lonely.[7]

The first time we stayed at the Mile Zero Motel, we were driving to a wedding in the Nazko Valley. That was the first day of the Mount McLean fire and we were uncertain whether it was a good idea to stay in Lillooet that night. We could see the flames on the mountainside, we could hear the crackling and explosion as trees candled and burned. A constant hum of activity as fire crews were dropped into the area and buckets of water were dumped from helicopters that carried them from the Fraser River flowing beneath the motel. But the town was lively so we decided to stay overnight. After checking in, we walked to the Greek restaurant for a very good dinner on a patio made cool with green vines. We drank golden retsina. After dinner we ambled along Main Street where many residents were sitting on lawn chairs arranged on the sidewalk, with coolers of beer and soft drinks beside them. It was like a parade but all the action was on the mountain—the helicopters edging close to flame, the smoke, huge plumes of orange flame, and the sizzle as water hit the hot spots. We hardly noticed the river.

A year or two later, in October, we returned to Mile Zero and its sad clean rooms. We had a little balcony off our standard queen and we sat on old chairs, drinking a glass of wine before heading out to dinner, and looking down on the wide Fraser River, and across where Simon Fraser observed "the metropolis of the Askeeih Nation."[8] It was a different river from the new green rush of water near Mount Robson. It was brown and steady, rippled like an animal, but not wild and turbulent. "This River, therefore, is not the Columbia," Fraser wrote sadly. "If I had been convinced of this fact where I left my canoes, I would certainly have returned from thence."[9] But we, who've seen both the Columbia and the Fraser, in different seasons, were happy to be there, sipping wine from the Fort Berens vines across the river, the grapes made plump with its waters.

In the morning, before an early start to Pavilion, we took a trail down below the railway tracks, through pines and sage, choke-cherry and small rocky gardens of prickly-pear cacti to the river's edge. There were deer tracks everywhere and what were these, the blackish-red piles of damp matter, still steaming? Ah, bear scat, with the whiff of the animal still in the air as it grazed on chokecherries just ahead of us. We returned to the trail and quietly ascended.

But to have seen the river in early light, close enough to dip our hands, to have skittered down the trail like returning deer, to have looked even briefly across this wide particular expanse while ospreys fell to the surface and rose with breakfast in their talons, was to continue the history of its watchers, its explorers, those who scavenge and forage on its banks, those who love its waters in every colour and tenor. The individual Nations that Simon Fraser passed through, with the kindnesses shown him, and still memory of him in places where people have lived for tens of thousands of years: "We had every reason to be thankful for our reception at this place."[10] Green, frothy aquamarine, bottle dark, olive green, brown. To have shared for a moment its loneliness, its virtue, its solitary madness while a bear ambled along its shimmering

length, eating cherries, was to be grateful for water, even as we followed the restless river again, passing the fishing ledges and chasms and the remnants of an ancient village in the grass at Keatley Creek, past the mountains Simon Fraser had described as "the most savage that can be imagined."[11] Of course he did not linger. Where in the river is its memory of its young beginnings, a trickle to make men ravenous for what they imagine it contains or promises? White sturgeon, Chinook, pink, sockeye salmon, trout and char, seals as far upriver as Yale, osprey, herons, gold, transport, dominion. Where in

the river is its privacy, its unknown side-channels, a place where a
person could wash up and begin again?

12 | *Nicola River, trail off Lauder Road, on the way to Glimpse Lake*

Driving to the Douglas Lake Ranch for ice cream and just to remind ourselves that some things remain, some trees, fencelines, horses (or the next generation), we saw the hoodoos on the other side of the Nicola River. Can we get to them, I wondered.

We turned off on Lauder Road and crossed a bridge over the river. It seemed there was a trail leading away from the chokecherries (and the bear scat) and spent shotgun shells by the cottonwoods. A dry trail, with dry cow pats, dry coyote scat brittle with little bones. And a few bones, too—the ribs of some large animal, probably a steer. A jaw. A few of the strange teeth wriggled in their sockets.

The river lithe and silver, skittish with small birds: swallows.

My muscles were so useful in those days. Walking the rough trail, my legs working well, my blood pumping, my heart strong. (There were signs of muscle damage in the bloodwork, the emergency room physician told me solemnly on the last trip to the hospital, the night we saw the cougar and heard water the whole way home, and I felt the weakness in my right knee, the cramping down my calf. The enzyme they found was creatine phosphokinase, I believe, and I hoped it wasn't my heart muscle that was damaged.) So, yes, useful, as we walked in intense heat. The hoodoos appeared but the trail dwindled away to almost nothing and we couldn't walk to their stony bases. A few wooden beams across a dry creekbed leading down to the river, the intense smell of sage stung with sunlight, withered mock orange blossoms on a few scattered bushes. In a deep pool, mayfly nymphs, floating twigs that were caddisfly larvae, dragonflies hovering in the air, their wings a screen for looking at the sun.

Uprooted cottonwood trees, an old fence post, earth from eroded riverbanks, impeding the flow of the water but somehow it found its way under and through while swallows dipped and turned.

The river came down through marshlands, entering Barton Lake, then Old Dave Lake, received its tributaries (Beak Creek and Frank Ward Creek), before flowing into Douglas Lake, then out again to run and riffle its way to Nicola Lake. A river of dry beautiful grasslands and the Spaxomin Reserve with its tumble of cabins and irrigation wheels turning through the hayfields on summer days. A river that leaves Nicola Lake, is controlled by a small dam at the south end, and passes the remnants of a sawmill (on Mill Creek, another small tributary) and a grist mill, on the river itself, and then meanders through ranchlands and brushy lowlands near Merritt, a series of oxbows making measurements difficult.

(Do leg veins oxbow, do they leave their established course and meander, in reaction to a blood clot? Do the femoral canals, the adductor canals, do they break down and allow various routes to collapse into a single moving blood flow to the lungs? Femoral to popliteal, veins and arteries going in their respective directions. I run my hands up and down my legs, wondering at their own strange rivers, their riparian zones, the floods or the droughts ahead.)

I have heard yellow-headed and red-winged blackbirds singing in the tule groves on the edges of the Nicola River where it leaves the lake on its way to the Thompson, taking in the Coldwater and Spius, the bodies of drowned cattle, a canoe left untethered as the river rose, and I have seen sandhill cranes flying overhead, the sound of them like creaking wagon wheels, and I've walked along the river's edge at dusk, behind the Upper Nicola townsite, once when we stayed in the old Banker's House and watched coho salmon swimming strongly towards the lake, so far from the ocean.

I have heard the blackbirds.

13 | *"I am haunted by waters."* [12]

The Green River as it meets the Colorado, the Tulameen entering
the Similkameen, the Granby and Kettle under the beautiful hills of
Grand Forks,

Early Winters Creek off the North Cascades Highway
coming into the Methow Valley, the Thames with its stories and
barges, a little quiet side channel of the Fraser where my father took
me as a child to see a huge sturgeon brought in by a local fisherman,
the Tagus as it empties

into the Atlantic near Lisbon,

the Chilcotin's milky-green at Bull Canyon (paintbrush, salsify, deep
blue larkspur, balsamroot and lupin),

the Yukon, the Tr'ondëk, the Danube and Elba,
the fast Rogue, the Red Deer, the Old Man, the Blackwater,
Bella Coola, Chute Creek, and Churn Creek, Soda Creek,

Williams Creek,

the Avon at Bradford where I watched the water from a stone bridge
dense with history, the Deadman and Bonaparte, Upper Hat Creek,

Coldwater, and the Kispiox where my children waded on a
hot day in July, the Leech and Jordan, the Nitinat and Koksilah, the
Oyster and Nimpkish, the Po (a rock, with an inscription, "Qui nasce
il Po," near Pian del Re, then the long journey to its fossil delta) and
Arno (where I stood on another bridge and wished I could afford soft
gloves) and the sweet Hoh, Queets, and Ozette where I camped as a
young woman, the Snake, the Escalante and Kanab, the Lost and the
Warm, and the Coeur d'Alene,

the Kern, the Mad, Klamath, and Rowdy Creek,

                              the Sooke, the Elk,

and the one I walk to season after season, near my home, where coho
salmon swim in by starlight

                    and mergansers wait to feed on their eggs.

14 | *Unbraided: a repair manual*

My physiotherapist tells me that the ligaments, bones, and cartilage exist in a relationship. He braids his fingers together to show me. Then he turns them askew, like my own braided hair after I've slept on it for a night or two, and he says our work will be to re-align the workings of my right leg. He doesn't think it's simply arthritis though he's breezily convinced that everyone over fifty has some degree of it in his or her joints. He speaks of trauma, of injury. A bump or a fall or a turn too far.

There's no hearing that I haven't bumped or fallen. That all of a sudden I had heat in my knee, an excess of fluid, terrible pain, and cramping. That the same thing had happened a year and a half ago, when I was diagnosed with a pulmonary embolism with no apparent cause, though deep vein thrombosis was suspected. (Double Doppler scans of my legs were clear, though it was thought the clot(s) had escaped, developed into the embolism and that's why there was no sign of further clots in my legs.) No hearing that I felt it was related to my body's response to pneumonia, to the difficult passage of the embolism travelling from my lower leg to my lungs. To the horror I felt when a respirologist thought that I had metastases in my lungs and ordered X-rays and bloodwork with tumour markers. The urgency at that time was to prevent further embolisms so the big drugs were employed. The specialists. The CT scans and the PET scan.

(There's no hearing.)

He braids his hands and turns them. He rubs my knee with an analgesic and runs an ultrasound wand over it. Then he shows me some exercises to do faithfully, three or five times a day. And I go home, thinking of how rivers break away and meet again, how they are the same, yet not. I stand facing the wall, bracing myself with my forearms, and stretch my leg behind me for fifteen seconds, then lift the opposite leg so that all the weight is on the stretched leg. I lie on my bed and hold my leg up, foot turned out like a ballet dancer, and my husband cradles my heel while I press down against the resistance of his hand. Five times. And it helps, it does, as regular swimming helps: my slow kilometre, I call it, three times a week. I envision the tissues and bones and gels finding each other again, remaking their tidy relationship. (I brush my hair and rebraid it in hope.) I want my physiotherapist's hands to show me that my body's geography has returned to the one I have known all my life. I want him to send a report to my doctor and I want her to tell me that the blood tests are normal and I want to think of my blood as flowing easily, without the difficult clots.

There was no fall, no collision. There was a time when I could walk easily, without pain; then two mornings, more than a year apart, when I couldn't. Just like that. What I returned to the first time wasn't normal but something between states. I hovered there, hover there still. There was a time I could walk easily.

Coda

Turn the page. Try to find the river you saw from a train window as you travelled from Avignon to Aix-en-Provence. Was it the Coulon? The Durance? Turn the page. There are photographs: the Nile Delta from space; a sunken church in Illinois as the Mississippi River flooded; the Colorado River dwindled to nothing as it approaches Mexico; the Slims River in the Yukon Territory, carrying meltwater from the Kaskawulsh Glacier, to the Kluane and eventually the Yukon River and the Bering Sea, now pirated by a shifting drainage gradient to the Gulf of Alaska. The diminishing South Saskatchewan.

Turn the page of your aging body and find the map of what might have happened.

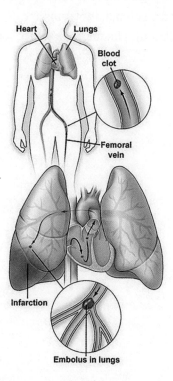

I wanted to know the route a deep vein thrombosis would take as it made its way to the lungs.
[Society for Vascular Surgery, Pulmonary Embolism. https://vascular.org/patient-resources/vascular-conditions/pulmonary-embolism]

Turn the page quickly. Remember the rivers you have walked along, and into, and how you were held by water green and lovely. How your grown sons still remember the Nicola River, your grown daughter the ride you took by horseback to Salmon River and its memory of the sockeye runs before the Hell's Gate slide in 1914, a river you have also driven along on your way to Salmon Arm, its silvery riffles so beautiful in sunlight. Before the slide and before bank erosion and flooding, agricultural run-off and the heavy feet of cattle making their way to water. (So many fish on this page, its wide waters.) How you stop at Lytton each trip to marvel again at the marriage of rivers, your husband's arm around your shoulders.

Turn the page. This atlas continues. Here are the maps of your legs and feet, a dense braiding of veins and arteries, blue, red, the multiple small tributaries finding their way to your heart, and back.

Blueprints

Noun
A design plan or other technical drawing.
Origin
Mid 19th century: from the original process in which prints were composed of white lines on a blue ground or of blue lines on a white ground.[1]

WHEN WE DECIDED we would build a house in 1980, we began with the question of how. John's mother still had the plans for the garage adjacent to the house she'd had built in Nanaimo a few years earlier and that seemed like a way to begin. Plans, free ones. Her garage was 16 feet by 24 feet. Let's do it, we said.

Between that moment and December 1982, when we moved into our house on the Sechelt Peninsula, not far from either Sakinaw Lake or Ruby Lake, a lot of things happened. To begin with, we didn't build a garage. John, who is thoughtful and practical (unlike me, who is headlong and, well, maybe a little visionary), talked to people, looked at the building code over and over until he knew what we needed to do in order to be given permits (which included hanging mirrors over sinks in bathrooms, a strange thing to be required). It became our second language. The code. What does the code require? Would it be to code? Ask at the building yard if 3/8s plywood is code.

So no garage, but those original dimensions—16×24—were the ones we used for the main rectangle we began with. John had decided that it would be easiest to think of a house in terms of connected rectangles and to make them interesting by varying levels and rooflines. We began with that first rectangle, then we built a second beside it, one step up—16×12—and another, of two storeys, behind: 20×20. The first rectangle would be the kitchen, a dining alcove, and an entrance area. The second rectangle would be the living room. The two-storey square would have two bedrooms (one intended for a study/guest room) and a bathroom on the first storey; the second storey would be a single large bedroom with a small ensuite bathroom at one end. A woodstove in the kitchen would provide most of the heat (with electric baseboards for back-up) and we'd keep areas as open as possible so that the heat could circulate through the rooms as well as rise to the second storey; there'd be no door at the top or bottom of the stairs. We'd install a ceiling fan to keep the warm air moving in winter, scooped down from the higher regions, and to cool the air in summer. A tasseled cord reversed direction, according to the season.

I have to say I was lost. I couldn't "see" any of these spaces. When John would ask at other people's houses if the room we were in was, oh, 12×16, he was relating space to basic plywood, which came in 4×8 sheets. There'd be less waste if we went with dimensions that were multiples of 4×8. He could make adjustments in his head, think his way through possible difficulties, and I'd be asking, Will there be a windowsill over the kitchen sink for my shells and stones? Can we have windows low in the dining area so we can see out while we're eating? My particulars were not his.

What also happened as we planned the rectangles—how high the windows, how wide the doors—was that we had a baby. While we built the first two rectangles, we lived in a blue tent raised on a plywood platform (two sheets; 8×8) with a tarp extending over it for added protection from coastal rain. The baby slept with us under our down sleeping bag in its duvet cover. I bathed him in the one enamelled tin basin we had in our camp kitchen (a homemade table under the tarp with a Coleman stove and a few battered saucepans), which was also our salad bowl, in water from Ruby Lake, brought up to the building site in a ten-gallon container. The well had yet to be drilled. The baby, who was Forrest, wore a toque at night because he had almost no hair.

And what happened before we moved into the three rectangles (because a square is also a rectangle) with their bare plywood floors and no doors to the bedrooms, was another baby, not quite born as we lugged our furniture and boxes of books and the entire contents of a kitchen into the house, but arriving soon after. The first baby was a toddler by then, eager to climb ladders, find abandoned nails in corners, and not careful enough around the woodstove so we constructed a corral from offcuts of 2×4s.

But this is all in the future. I am putting the house and its life before the drawings that conceived it. I want to write about the blue-prints. How John drew rooms onto big sheets of paper, using special rulers and other measures, representing lintels, top-plates, the distances between windows, how a door might open in, or out, and how a life unfolds from what a pencil projects.

• • • • • •

In the early nineteenth century, Anna Atkins used a process of sun-printing, with paper soaked in ferric ammonium citrate and potassium ferricyanide, to make cyanotypes of British algae, ferns, and flowering plants. Her prints are beautiful, fusing scientific observation and artistic arrangement, and they set a standard for photography that influenced many who came after her, though their processes were perhaps more sophisticated. She was the first woman to make a book of her images—her self-published *Photographs of British Algae* appeared in 1834. Yet who remembers her, apart from a few historians?[2]

Iris sibirica, Pteris aquilina, Ophioglossum vulgatum (the adder-tongue fern), *Equisetum sylvaticum*, fertile and sterile stems both, curving in such elegance I can imagine Anna's hands arranging them, and maybe my favourite of the algae, the delicate *Chordaria flagelliformis,* sprawled across the page like a fine map of capillaries, I imagine Anna's hands washing the paper after its exposure to sunlight, watching the image appear. As though the sky itself had lent its colours, the images not white exactly but a faint blue, perfectly clear, on indigo cloth.

· · · · · ·

There was a shop in Brno I passed when I walked from my hotel to the university where I was teaching for a week. I peered through windows at shelves filled with Czech folk pottery, dolls, textiles, and bolts of dark blue cotton printed in white. I've always loved blue, am drawn to it as a pigment, as a dye, as fabric, soft clothing (I've always worn my blue jeans until they've fallen apart), tiles, ceramics, decorative or functional, the blue flowers that are often so difficult to grow. Delphiniums in my garden are routinely eaten by slugs, hydrangeas by deer, though the prettiest blue of all, the small forget-me-nots thrive where they aren't necessarily wanted, tiny yellow eyes at their centre, and blue poppies, so lovingly grown from seed by a friend, don't thrive here in my garden, forty-five minutes north of his.

At the shop in Brno, I'd linger by the window, entering once to purchase two little pieces of the blue patterned ceramics to take to people who'd kindly hosted me on my travels. It didn't occur to me to buy a few metres of the fabric.

And then I was given a small tablecloth made of the cotton. I was told by my new Czech friend as she handed me the package that it was Moravian blueprint or modrotisk. The cotton had a kind of patina almost. I wanted to know more about it but the woman who gifted it to me didn't have any information. Later on my travels, I was taken to the Wallachian Open Air Museum in Rožnov pod Radhoštěm. In the area where we bought our tickets, there were a few souvenirs of the district. I was thrilled to find bolts of the modrotisk and bought a metre each of the two patterns available.

I didn't have time then to find out about the process of creating the deep blue ground printed with white but once home, I discovered that clean starched cotton is printed with wooden blocks surface-coated with a resist paste, allowed to dry, then the cloth is dipped in indigo dye repeatedly to achieve the deep blue. The cloth is then washed in weak sulphuric acid to remove the paste that has kept the printed areas white. The cloth is rinsed and pressure is applied, via mangle, to give the surface a lustre (or patina) that makes it almost glow. Further patina can be achieved by polishing the fabric with stones.

I loved learning about the process. It echoed what I already knew about Japanese resist indigo dyeing, katazome, and in some ways the stylistic elements resemble one another. I read a fair bit about both traditions and can find no evidence that one grew out of the other; both evolved continents away, but reveal what might almost be hard-wired into human textile workers: a love for blue and white pattern. In Africa, there is also a long tradition of indigo textiles; the vats at Kofar Mata in Nigeria have been used since the early sixteenth century. The end product is beaten with wooden implements to achieve the polished results similar to both the modrotisk and katazome. I have indigo-dyed cloths from India, too, with resist patterns skillfully applied. One of them could almost be a design by Anna Atkins, the blue ground printed with two kinds of leaves.

I've done some indigo dyeing myself, sort of carelessly but lovingly, and have made quilts with the results. Sometimes I create resist patterns with beach stones or by using wood and clamps or by tying lengths of fabric with hemp cord. I've bound lengths around PVC pipe, painted fish onto cloth with melted wax to create a resist pattern, onto other lengths of cloth, and sewn long parallel lines with dental floss to pull tight to create the mokume, or woodgrain, pattern. What I end up with is never very impressive but I love the sense that I am partic-ipating in the process of taking cloth to a three-dimensional state and then back to two-dimensional after the dyeing, removing stones, ironing out wax stitching, thread, clamped wood, and knowing that the pattern is the cloth remembering that third dimension. The quilt I made using a length of rough linen strewn with snow angels or stars, created with stones from Trail Bay in Sechelt, dreams of those stones as it lies folded on the back of a couch, backed with soft red flannel, fabric that has known other shapes, other weather (I dyed it on a summer morning while pileated woodpeckers taught their young to feed), and dreams of children in snow, arms fluttering like wings.

I've never polished my fabric with stones or wooden hammers. My quilts and tablecloths achieve their patinas via daily or celebratory use, washing, sunlight, spills of wine as guests toast the season, the cook (who is usually me), the occasion of all of us gathering together. Oops, a ladle of sauce from the lamb shanks dribbled the whole length of the table. A glass is knocked, buttered bread falls in a predictable way. The stains that are left become part of a larger pattern, never intended when I tied stones into knots with string or elastic bands, but welcomed nevertheless. What is the dimension when memory calls every dinner into being? Every birthday? Every lingering conversation over dessert? It is the dimension I enter when I plunge cloth into dye, when I untie it, when I sew by the fire, when I spread a quilt on a bed for a guest. A blueprint for the years, using techniques the hands remember, fingers blue-stained from the work.

· · · · · ·

Blueprint questions and answers[3]

1. How did you begin to figure out how to draw the plans for our house? How did you know how to represent space, perspective, dimension?

> I honestly can't remember* the details of how I did the actual drawings. I've had a piece of brown-stained good-one-side plywood with a little ledge on one long edge kicking around for years and I think I might have used it as a surface, taping the large paper sheets down and using a T-square to keep all the horizontal lines parallel. Then the verticals would all be at right angles to them. As you know I did buy a three-sided ruler with scale options on it and chose the three-eighths-inch to one-foot scale. And I remember getting the proper pencils. There's no perspective in the drawings. So that's why the roofs appear to be foreshortened, the height to the

peaks from the eaves is to scale so you have the four in twelve (four feet of height to twelve feet of horizontal distance, proportionately) lift of the roofs indicated in the drawings, not the distance from the eaves to the peaks.

(I stopped reading to puzzle through what he meant: a lack of perspective.)

I do remember much more clearly some basic precepts I worked with in the planning, the most useful being the suggestion to plan room sizes (and exterior wall sizes, overall dimensions) in eight-foot increments. This is because plywood, for floor and wall sheathing, and drywall for interior wall and ceiling finish, comes in eight-foot by four-foot sheets and planning to those dimensions saves a lot of waste in off-cut and a lot of time. Also the optimal spacing for floor and ceiling joists and wall studs is sixteen inches on centre, because those multiples fit exactly into four-foot increment spaces. Carpenter tape-measures all have the sixteen-inch centres in red on them. So it was a no-brainer to plan two rectangular elements to the original building, one sixteen by twenty-four, the other sixteen by twelve. I didn't want the structure to look like a long box so two rectangles off-set gave it some character, and I changed levels between the two because I knew we were going to expand backward later from the smaller rectangle and the grade went uphill in that direction, so as well as getting the contrast in elevation I could follow the grade and avoid having to blast out granite to get enough height for the addition. Aesthetically the change in height indoors was a way to break up large open-plan spacing, and to differentiate between rooms but still allow easy distribution of heat from a single woodstove, for example.

What has all this to do with blueprints? I was no good at all in drafting or art at school. Necessity made a very rudimentary draftsman of me but the drawings were just for the bureaucrats and permits really. I could easily follow the principles and requirements of the building code without to-scale plans. As we did for a number of building projects later...

(*Later, he remembered he used graph paper for the drafts.)

2. How many drafts did it take to come up with the final versions?

Can't remember but I do remember a lot of erasing!

3. When you look at the plans now, how do you feel? What do you remember about drawing them?

They make me proud a little. I did what I had to do to build a good house. As you know we tried to do everything that we could ourselves. There was pretty standard advice among builders about doing things yourself; most mistakes could easily be corrected if you were careful and patient; best to leave finishing tasks like mudding drywall to the experts as it took a couple of houses to get any good at it and you'd always be looking at it. I could add another directive I came up with myself: Jobs requiring specialized tools and skills were best left to the pros. But there aren't very many of those. For me I stayed clear of high roofs but was okay roofing on lower, smaller roofs, especially applying shakes. I wasn't about to try to do torch-on rolled roofing or the like. Similarly, roughing-in plumbing had messy chemical sealants and awkward angles to work with and seemed too much to learn when I was in a hurry to get on with finishing the building. Surprisingly, electrical wiring was straightforward, mostly indoors during the bad weather and only a small-bore wood drill and a pair of wire-stripping pliers required.

Seeing the plans make me sad too, that it was all so long ago. What a project we took on!

• • • • • •

She wrote with seaweed

Anna Atkins collected botanical specimens for Kew Gardens. She helped to illustrate her father's translation of Lamarck's *Genera of Shells*. She was given a camera in 1841, though I believe no examples of her standard photographs survive. She learned to make cyanotypes and made hundreds of images, relying on her excellent scientific mind to capture algae and ferns and flowers in all their intricate beauty. Her work was consistently good and she obviously paid careful attention to the timing of the cyanotypes because the Prussian blue of the paper is always clear and fine. I think of my own attempts to achieve the perfect blue when I dip my cloth into indigo dye and how easily I am distracted from the clock by woodpeckers, mosquitoes stinging the small of my back, the urgent growling of my stomach, the knowledge that household tasks await me indoors. I move the hoses in the garden, stop to pull a few weeks, deadhead roses, and realize I've forgotten to remove the tied cloth bundles from their vat of dye.

But Anna! She wrote her captions in delicate seaweeds. Her blue-prints are a hoard of perfect quilt blocks waiting to be arranged and stitched. They are scraps of summer sky. They are a world made perfect, young algae, fruiting examples, a dreamworld, a blue heaven, where the tiniest plants float through a blue sea, nothing to damage them, almost two hundred years old and as alive as anything I've ever seen.

Fucus vesiculosus, Polypodium vulgare, Leucojam varium, Cystopteris dentata, Asplenium septentrionale, Punctaria latifolia, Botrychium lunaria, blue paper haunted with their images, as I am haunted by them, by a woman who sought, identified, collected, and dried plants, immersed sheets of paper in ferric ammonium citrate and potassium ferricyanide, arranged the plants, set glass over them, positioned them in sunlight, timed, waited, rinsed the sheets in clear water, and left a vast garden of white on blue for us to wonder at centuries after.

• • • • • •

What a project we took on, he wrote in answer to my questions. He did the plotting, the imagining, pencilling in details that he erased, pencilled in, erased again. In his mind, stacks of 2×4 studs, sheets of plywood, larger timbers for the joists and beams. And before that, concrete made in a red wheelbarrow (irony never commented on by a man who loved William Carlos Williams, or at least never in my memory), poured into boxes framed out of 2×6s or 2×8s, or else Sonotube, rebar carefully placed to allow us to anchor the posts once the concrete had set. Load after load mixed with a shovel, cement, sand and gravel, and water we brought up from the lake in ten-gallon containers. And before that, the site cleared of debris, measurements taken, holes dug to grade for the footings, batter-boards at each corner with string and a line level and a plumb-bob to ensure everything would be square. What a project as we rocked our baby to sleep at night on one chest or another. Coffee made in the morning on the Coleman stove and a campfire to keep the bugs away. From a blueprint, we built a house, though as John said, "I could easily follow the principles and requirements of the building code without to-scale plans." He could. I couldn't. I couldn't see the line of the roof from the drawings, the spatial relationships, how it would look when we moved in with our little boy and another nearly ready to be born. I hoped for the best.

• • • • • •

They spelled my grandfather's name incorrectly on the bill he received from J.W. Doze for surveying work on the land he seems to have owned with my grandmother and two other couples, in Beverly, Alberta, in 1954. Well, by then he owned a portion of the land subdivided a year earlier. I have the blueprint of the plan showing the subdivision of Lot c Block 6 Plan 2528 A R in Beverly Heights Annex, Lot E Block 39 Plan 7242 A H in Beverly Heights, and part of Lot A Block 5 Plan 2528 A R Beverly Heights Annex, River Lot 38 and 40 Beverly.

The bill is made out to Mr. Kirskan. I'm not surprised. I have the same surname and know how frequently it's misspelled, by mistake or deliberately. I say my name clearly and almost always spell it, as a courtesy. I know my grandfather spoke English with a heavy Ukrainian accent. I know that his wife, my grandmother Anna, was called Annie on her naturalization and Canadian citizenship papers. Did she choose to be called the diminutive form of her dignified name? I suspect not. The records of her life in the country she left list her as Anna. But my grandparents' lives were diminished in small ways, and large ones, by the country they arrived at with no English, very little money, but such hope.

I've tried to figure out a sequence for the land purchase, the house they arranged to relocate from Humberstone Farm, and the house they built. I have a handwritten bill of sale, for $200, signed by Jacob Prins on February 8, 1946, for the former, which had to be moved on or before the first day of July, 1946. I have a building permit issued by the Town of Beverly on April 8, 1946 for a house to be built on Lot E Block 39 Plan 7242 A H. That information aligns with the house that I remember and have found since, on 111th Avenue in Beverly, still standing, though I didn't see the little house I also remember, the one we slept in when we visited our grandparents, the one with the tin roof.

Who were Peter and Pearl Pawliuk? Who were John and Annie Walrich(k)? In 1953, their names and their awkward signatures, or marks, appear on the blueprint of the subdivision plan, along with my grandparents' signatures. Anna (she is Anna in her own writing) and John Kishkan. Were they business partners or friends who might also have moved to Beverly from Drumheller when my grandparents moved, when work dried up in the mines there, and who knows, maybe the Prins connection had to do with my grandfather's work as a coal miner. The Humberstone Farm was located nearby, it seems, the original owners William and Beata Humberstone buying a half section of River Lot 42, east of 34th Street and south of 118th Avenue early in the twentieth century, farming part of the land and operating a coal mine on part of it. The Prins family bought the property sometime after 1927. As well as farming and selling coal, both families boarded miners so perhaps the little house my grandparents bought was surplus after the coal operations slowed down.

On the back of the bill for survey work, there are three quavery attempts at a signature: my grandfather's. He was illiterate, my father always said, and my father also said he'd taught his father to sign his name. So here's the proof, the practise signatures, one of them complete and two of them trailing off after the "h" in Kishkan. On the blueprint, my grandparents' signatures look suspiciously alike. Did my grandmother sign for both of them? Beside John and Annie Walrich(k)'s names, both looking as though they are also from the same hand, is a note, beside two squiggles: his mark; her mark.

Yet whatever skills these people didn't have—graceful signatures, a confident ability to tell others their names and how to spell them, the dignity of clear language—they owned land. They paid their bills. Received payment May 25th/54, notes J.W. Doze on his bill. Paid by cash $200, on the bill of sale signed by J. Prins and witnessed by (it looks like N., for Jacob's son Norman?) Prins. Other receipts, for insurance; for building supplies and services (including electrical work—outlets, service insulators, outlet and wiring for the chicken house from the firm of Prins-Sagert & Co.); payment in full ($300.80) for stucco, signed by Fred Blanchard on October 17/46; taxes, also paid promptly.

I saved all these scraps of paper and the big blueprint, having found them in various old folders and envelopes, unsorted, stained with coffee marks and age, after my father died in 2009. He too had saved them. What can we know about a life, *lives*, by reading the old pencil marks on bills of sale? Someone has tried to provide an estimate for building (a house, the house they had built in 1946?), tried to detail with some asperity the concept of materials and labour: "Laber you have to figer how much cost to build house...Eletric cost, fixchers in house." There is much I don't understand.

So I have the blueprint showing the land divided into neat geometrical shapes, the signatures and marks of people who must have been friends or even relatives, and I know where my grandparents' home was located on the blueprint. I know that they already lived on a corner lot and that they'd built a house, had moved another house (referred to in that building estimate by the person whose spelling skills were only marginally better than theirs as a "shack") from Humberstone Farm, though how that happened I can't imagine: a horse-drawn wagon? A flat-bed truck easing down their road with children watching and maybe a dog chasing the wheels? I do imagine a warm day, bottles of beer brought out to the workers, and maybe a plate of my grandmother's cheese pastries. A tiny glass of slivovice to seal the deal. I don't see steps to the front door in the photograph I took of the house on a trip to Beverly with my granddaughter last year but my older brother remembers sitting on a stoop, eating corn with our grandfather. A house can change over the decades and our accumulation of family memories adjusts to the years, ours and theirs.

Like the Moravian modrotisk that was made in my grandmother's area of what's now the Czech Republic, an image is impressed with durable paste, and pressure. Washed and washed and washed over time, the cloth might fade but someone will recall the beauty of white on deep blue, the marks of two people who knew little English but were careful, paid their bills on time, and lived frugally so that their son, my father, might have a better life. Could they ever have imagined my life now, with my own set of blueprints to puzzle through and try to remember how dimensions were determined, how my husband sat at a desk with an improvised drafting table in front of him, planning the rooms that would hold our lives? How it felt to lift heavy joists to the walls so that the beams had support, to give a bedroom its final coat of paint, to move a stove into place, lay a rug on the plywood floor of the living room? Impossible questions but I ask them, to keep in my own being the threads of our connection, however faded and frayed. I was a little girl to them, a child who hugged the old woman in a rocking chair on a low porch in Edmonton. Who may have resembled their only surviving child, or not. Dark-haired, like my grandfather, dark-eyed like the young bride my grandmother was in the first photograph I saw of her, her hair in a neat bun and a small smile on her face as she stood beside her new husband, who died too young, leaving her alone in Drumheller with nine children, soon to be eight. Her second husband, my grandfather, had not yet entered the picture.

He made the drawings. He sat at the desk overlooking Burrard Inlet after his teaching job finished for the day, putting aside his poems. He made marks, erased, used the three-sided ruler I sometimes take out for special quilt measurements. (Nothing is wasted but repurposed.) He rolled the big sheets of paper with our house carefully imagined, no perspective, nor the distance from the eaves to the peak, but a means to see our way to building the platforms, the walls sheathed in plywood, the joists and beams to carry our roof aloft, and he took them to a place off Marine Drive in North Vancouver where they were reproduced by the process that replaced blueprint (not unlike the process used by Anna Atkins to preserve what she loved in white lines on blue paper, the negative image of what she placed on a page in sunlight). The term "blueprint" is still used for reproductions of architectural drawings and floor plans, though when John took our drawings to the office to have copies made, the process was a form of xerography. No longer Prussian blue, no longer a page of sky showing how a house might be viewed from an angle impossible for me to apprehend. Now we'd probably hold a phone or my small Samsung tablet, loaded with plans we could zoom in on, scroll, turn to see alternate views. There would be perspective. Looking at the little screen, we'd determine the dimensions of the lumber we needed to cut and piece together to make a house. A home.

• • • • • •

Anna Atkins left her herbarium to the British Museum in 1865, six years before her death. Occasionally her cyanotypes are exhibited in major galleries and museums. I imagine a room hung with her seaweeds and ferns, the delicate *Iris sibirica*, white plants in a blue heaven. Hers is a body of blueprint that has lasted, a sublime garden she has left for us in the future, reduced to two colours. We can turn the page of her garden wherever we are. In a gallery. In our house, drawn first in pencil, three-eighths-inch to one-foot scale, no perspective, the roofs foreshortened. Yet our perspective is measured by huge Douglas firs, a dip where the lake is, a mountain beyond, and beyond that, Agamemnon Channel where it meets Georgia Strait, Texada Island in the blue distance. And my own perspective through time is measured by how much I remember or can deduce from the sheaf of papers left by my father, all that is left of his parents' household: a small building on 111th Avenue in Beverly, within spitting distance of the North Saskatchewan River. Listen. Listen. You can hear the ice breaking up as I write, the sound of magpies in the old cottonwoods. Let's go there. I'll spread out a cloth of modrotisk on the rough grass and we can stretch out on that plain ground, an old honeycomb of coalmines under us as we share a cool drink and think of this blue world we inhabit, we try to record, we keep in any way that we can.

Anatomy of a Button

WHEN I FINISHED PIECING TOGETHER my quilt top made up of small rectangles of various cottons and silks, the one I named "A Dark Path" for the process of making it in January and February after I'd fallen on ice a few weeks before Christmas and, as a result of the impact of the fall, torn my retinas, well, I let the top sit in my quilting basket because I didn't know what do with it next.

I was seeing the ophthalmologist every two weeks. At first I went to him and he found the tear that an ophthalmology resident in Edmonton had suspected after examining my eyes in early December when I'd been taken to Emergency at the Royal Alexandra Hospital during a blizzard because I'd been seeing cascades of silvery stars and streaks to one side of my vision. The ophthalmologist confirmed the tear, repaired it with a laser procedure, asked me to come back in two weeks as a follow-up, then again later in January just to make sure everything was fine. And it wasn't. There were two more tears, which he repaired. I returned for follow-up a few more times and on March 25th, I was told I was no longer at risk.

I put my mind to the quilt top. What would I do with it? It was made in the boro tradition. Rather than piece rectangles together by sewing right sides together and then turning and pressing each seam, I cut a big piece from an old cotton sheet and laid out a path down the middle third of the cotton, finding the most pleasing way to arrange

A clean oyster shell holding buttons, faces looking up, eyes luminous with life.

the small scraps of mostly blue fabric. Using a long sashiko needle, threaded with dark blue embroidery floss, I sewed the scraps onto the cotton with running stitches, letting the fraying edges of the fabric remain.

The ophthalmologist showed me a chart of the eye. He showed me where the retina lines the back wall of the eye, a nerve layer that senses light and creates electrical impulses that are sent to the brain. There's a large mass of jelly in front of the retina called the vitreous humour and as we get older, it liquifies a bit. No big deal, he said, but in your case, the impact of your fall caused the vitreous to tug at your retinas. And your retinas tore as a result. Luckily this was discovered by the resident and her recommendation that you seek medical attention as soon as possible meant we could repair the first tear. Quite honestly, we didn't expect the next two. But the vitreous has eased away now and no longer has traction with the retina so it's unlikely you will have any more problems. But you were lucky. Your retinas could have detached completely and then it would be far more serious. You could have sustained a permanent degree of visual loss or even become blind.

Somehow the dark path of scraps finding their way down the middle of a piece of old sheet helped me to think about how vulnerable I'd felt, and how lucky. You try to find your footing on a perilous path and you carefully step from one stone to another until you've reached the end of the path. I used two lengths of fabric, one a piece of deep blue silk with woven teal medallions that had come with a box of old recycled kimonos I'd ordered, thinking I could cut them for quilts (I couldn't, but that's another story), and one a piece of Japanese indigo cotton, printed with white crosshatches, sewing them lengthwise on either side of the path. I had a finished top 43 inches wide by 65 inches long.

Now what? I'd come through the experience with my sight intact but with scars at the backs of my eyes from the laser procedures. Quite often I'd lay my hands gently over my eyes and imagine a life without sight. There are worse things, I know, but I thought of everything I loved to look at—tulips, birds in flight, favourite landscapes, the sky (particularly the late February sky at 6:30 p.m. on a fine day when it's the blue of Maxfield Parrish paintings, sometimes with Venus and a new moon hanging silver above the Douglas firs), the faces of those I love (an increasing number of people because of grandchildren), prairie fields from a great height (flying from the coast to Ottawa and back), freshly washed sheets fluttering on the clothesline in wind, the chartreuse flowers on bigleaf maples, and so many more things—and I'd realize how grateful I was that I wasn't blind. Sometimes I'd hold my hands over my eyes for a bit longer because I was crying.

A couple of weeks after my final ophthalmology appointment, I arranged to see an optometrist because my vision had changed a little after the experience of having my retinas damaged and repaired. I could no longer read easily in bed at night without straining to see the text on the page. I have a good reading lamp and I've read in bed all my life, often for two hours or more; I rarely watch television and books are what I look forward to at the end of the day. A technician took photographs of my inner eyes and when I was sent on to the optometrist's office, she had those images on her screen. After routine procedures, she showed me my eyes. Here, and here, and here, she pointed. Those are where your retinas were repaired. Little scars like buttons sealed my retinas in place.

On my way home, I knew what I'd do with the quilt top. I had a length of teal dupioni silk, just enough for the backing. I had batting but did I really need to use batting for this quilt? It wasn't going to be used on a bed. It was kind of fragile, though I didn't intend it to be. Boro means "tattered"; the technique is used to mend and continue the life of clothing by patching with scraps of cloth, and those scraps are part of a long story of a garment, a family, a history of use. Boro clothing and bedcovers are warm, often layered over time, and the layers are held together with sashiko stitching; sashiko means "little stabs." The stitching is intended to be structural rather than decorative but as is so often the case, structural and practical become beautiful when done carefully and well. My path isn't skillful and I suspect the structure isn't all that strong. But I think it's beautiful and it's a visual representation of a dark period. My husband and I were reading Dante's *Inferno* and I wasn't talking much about my fears because my husband had his own and I didn't want to add to his anxiety. But sewing, I knew, in a seriously profound way, that I'd found myself in a dark wood and maybe I wasn't out of the woods yet. I felt strangely strong, resolute. I just needed to find my own path in and through and out the other side.

So I cut the dupioni silk to size. I wouldn't use batting. I'd find a way to secure the top to the back without complicating the simple pattern of the path leading down the centre of the quilt. Maybe I'd use buttons, though I wasn't sure how I'd arrange them.

Years ago I fell in love with akoya buttons, made from the shells of *Pinctada fucata,* an oyster from the Indo-Pacific region, used for the culture of pearls. The buttons are made from the nacre or mother-of-pearl lining of the shells after the pearls are gathered. I discovered a tiny store on Homer Street in Vancouver that sells the buttons in many sizes; they're used primarily by First Nations artists making button blankets. The blankets, specific to Nations of the Northwest Coast, are worn for ceremonial purposes and were originally decorated with dentalium and small squares of abalone shell outlining crests. Imagine them in firelight, shimmering, bringing the family crests to light. When traders provided pearl buttons, they were used in place of the abalone, though the button store sells abalone buttons as well as akoya. The abalone buttons are greener than akoya, which are silvery, and the abalone are much more expensive; the populations of many of the subgenera are at risk and harvesting them is prohibited, though some species are farmed, and one—the red abalone, *Haliotis rufescens*—is subject to a restricted sport fishery in California. I buy buttons by the hundreds, which is the most economical way to acquire them. They come in many sizes and I buy whatever sizes I think will work for projects I haven't even imagined yet. Tiny as lentils to buttons the size of a quarter, though they come even larger. I've used them on quilts of batiked salmon on indigo ground: I use a single small button for the eyes and then a few along the spine. I've also scattered tiny buttons among the stones I've batiked along the grounds of these quilts, to suggest bubbles and eggs. I've finished stitched spirals with single buttons of various sizes. For this quilt, I was thinking of strewing buttons in a random way along the dark path—stones on the trail, moments of light, and in the most practical terms, a way of securing the layers together, as the lasers secured my retinas to the backs of my eyes.

The earliest known button is 5,000 years old and was found in the Indus Valley. It was made of shell. The more things change and evolve, the more sophisticated we believe our material culture to be, the more we find out that people have always wanted to fasten clothing with objects that are beautiful. To fasten one thing to another or simply to exist as a thing of beauty. Five thousand years ago, the people of the Indus Valley had measuring sticks of ivory marked out with decimals, they had stepped ponds, with descending stairs to the water surface, where people congregated for practical and ceremonial purposes. The oldest known button was whorled on one surface, flat on the other. Some people believe that buttons in the Indus Valley civilization were used solely for sartorial decoration. But is this surprising? I think of the times I've replaced plain buttons on a piece of clothing with filigreed metal ones or akoya ones gleaming in the light or carved wooden ones. When I go to the button shop to replenish my quilting buttons, I have to restrain myself from also choosing carved fish or tiny ceramic Venus of Willendorfs or swirling marbled discs I would sew onto a beret. If I wore a beret.

After my visit to the optometrist, I come home thoughtful. I have seen my inner eye with its small scars, discs securing my retinas in place. I have a dark path of silk and linen and indigo cotton and I have a basket of akoya buttons that I run my thumb over as I shake a few into an oyster shell to see how I might use them on this quilt. I imagine the process of stamping the buttons out of shells and then seeing them sized and polished, drilled with holes (mine all have two holes, though I've seen them with four), left loose or sewn onto cards for distribution to stores. I consider my thread.

Sinew, gut, veins, threaded through holes in needles made of bone or tied securely to one end, guided through hide and fur, 30,000 to 60,000 years ago, and possibly longer. Plant fibres, twisted and turned until a strong thread was ready to attach one thing to another, snares and nets and fasteners created to hold clothing to the body, tying the knot, using a well-knapped flint to cut the end. In Greek mythology, the Moirai or sisters of Fate spun the threads of our lives, measured them to determine the length of our lives, and cut them to end our time on earth. The threads of our past, our present, and our future spun, and measured, and cut with shears. We know something of this cycle in our own bodies: we are born, the cord connecting us to our mothers cut, our days measured out, our own children born out of our bodies, those cords cut and tied off to make them separate from us, the large artery of our heart distributing oxygenated blood until it can no longer keep us alive. Maybe we have sewn, maybe we have threaded needles, pushed them through cloth, gathered and smoothed and trimmed the threads, and we have sewn buttons, mended tears in our clothing or our children's clothing, patched and layered, we have drawn cord through a seam and pulled the cord tight until the opening closed and whatever we had gathered in a bag was safe for now. Maybe we have put our mending aside and waited for a quieter moment, sunlight on our favourite chair. A clean oyster shell holding buttons, faces looking up, eyes luminous with life.

When I take up the quilt, I hear the silk rustling. It is almost alive under its top of patches and panels. Rustling like bird wings, something I could hear with my eyes closed. If I close my eyes, I hear the silk, the sound of rain on the roof, the restless movement of the cat investigating the boxes behind my desk. I push my thread through the holes in the shell buttons, two eyes side by side, tender stabs with a sharp needle. For a moment a tiny button hangs on the thread as I fiddle with a tangled bit, trying to ease it out. By a thread. We hang by a thread in this world of wonders and terror. On a path of indigo cotton, black silk streaked with gold, squares of grey flannel, linen the colour of midnight, these silvery buttons will make a small light for anyone walking in uncertainty, in hope, scarred or whole, the whole dark length.

Love Song

ON AN EARLY SUMMER MORNING, I wake to the sound of Swainson's thrushes. Beyond my bedroom window, beyond the house, they sing where the woods begin. And there are robins, vireos, the long whistle of a varied thrush. My curtains are rough white linen and they filter light, the light at dawn, coming from the east, pink and golden as the sun finds its way over Mount Hallowell. My husband sleeps closest to the window and he pulls the curtains aside to let in more song. There is honeysuckle blooming, and dog roses, trumpet vines. Hummingbirds bury themselves in the flowers. The pink throats of the tree frogs inflate, a loud vibrato close enough to touch. A face peers in the window through the lattice of vines and it's a weasel, as surprised to see me in a bed with pillows and a log-cabin quilt as I am to see a weasel among the dog roses. That's what I've been hearing, I tell my husband, the sound I've been hearing racing along the eaves-troughs, wondering at the light-footed speed. Going out the French doors to the deck, I see a weasel slink into the ridge of flashing where the sunroom roof meets the wall of the house, its body as sinuous as water. It's hunting mice for its young. And anything else small and slow-moving. Already a robin nest has been emptied of its eggs.

The light is our clock. We talk quietly in bed, listening to the birds. In the night there were loons and we're glad they've chosen the bay below us for nesting. One of us remembers a summer when the house was filled with children. Another remembers waking in the tent to face a day of house-building, framing and lifting walls, running out of nails, measuring and measuring again the bird's mouth notches so that the rafters would rest snugly on the wall plates. One baby slept in a basket on the sleeping bag in the blue tent. (The others were still unborn, waiting to be dreamed into being.) One baby slept in a crib in the new wing of the house, in a room next to the one with bunk beds, while I walked in the garden in a cotton nightdress, coaxing the peas to attach themselves to wire. Three children didn't sleep as the sun set later and later, long past bedtime, and we made campfires in rings of stones, sat on a cedar plank while the smoke rose to the stars. In the garden, the sundial (*Grow Old With Me, The Best is Yet to Come*) was smothered by lemon balm.

On the Solstice, the sun finds its rising place a little to the north of true east and when it sets, it's north of west. More than sixteen hours of light. How often we use our finger to point to the west and find the place where the sun sets in February, in June, in September. As the earth orbits, the light shifts. And our orbit shifts—up early with the sun to begin the watering, to weed and tie up and move plants, and to pick the evening's salad before the heat turns the soft leaves bitter. To note aphids and scale insects. To take a few minutes to cut roses and flowering sage for the table. One son has left for his job at the library, another sleeps off his late night at the local restaurant where he clears tables and washes dishes over the lengthy dinner period. A daughter is preparing for Guide camp.

Out in the boat with a picnic to eat on the island in the lake, the island we call White Pine for the little grove on its high point, or else "Going to Greece" for the scent of yarrow and dry grass. I spread out a bamboo mat on the spine of the hill and brush ants from my legs while one child dives from the rocks and another swims underwater. The third is learning to start the boat motor, pulling the cord and adjusting the choke. One son brings his wife and baby—but wait, it's too early for this: the picnic first, and the last years of high school, the long years of university, a wedding still a decade to come. Two weddings. Far out in the lake, a merganser leads her ducklings to the mouths of small trout-haunted creeks where insects are plentiful. The boat makes two trips or three to take all the people who have come with the years, the old picnic basket filled to the brim. A black dog with the hips of a wolf hangs over the prow, eager for land.

There are calzones in the basket and tins of sparkling lemonade; later, bottles of cider, cool from the shallows where they've been corralled with rocks. How long can a girl dive before her father accords her a perfect score, how many times can a boy circumnavigate the island with the throttle on low? Another practises the dead man's float. Three years, or six. Drift on a raft under the low-growing spirea and bog laurel, count turtles on logs, crush a few leaves of wild mint in your hands while the years accumulate. Nine years, or twelve.

My curtains are rough white linen and they filter moonlight. Some evenings I still walk out in my cotton nightdress to pluck slugs from the lettuces, watch for deer who bring their fawns to eat rose canes escaping the fence. How many generations of deer, how many of bears lying in wait for the apples to ripen as they turn over stones on the path for the abundance of ants? Four, or seven, or thirty-two. And even the dogs, long dead, are racing in circles around the garden fence. One of them loved blackberries, one ate salal from the bushes along the driveway. In the dense woods a varied thrush adjusts its pitch, another answers from the understory. The robin nest is filled again with soft blue eggs. The weasel has yet to appear by the window, though the curtains are now open, the roses are blooming.

And now it's time, the sundial showing itself beneath a tangle of green leaves smelling of lemon and loud with bees, the yellow-faced, orange-rumped, Sitka, and western. The table is set; time to come up from the lake. Old songs play on the stereo, the ones we've sung all these years in summer. You can't hurry love. Come along, your bodies cool, duck-itchy, the baby fat turned to muscle, your own children in your arms as you scatter damp towels and hang bathing suits on the railings. Friends are bringing food from their cars, even the ones who've died and are remembered on birthdays or the anniversary of a wake. Here they are, with their dishes of tomatoes, prawns, skewers of chicken, the familiar brownies dusted with icing sugar.

They are standing on the patio where the young robins are learning to fly, where the lizards cross from woodshed to stones in the blink of an eye. I've waited forever to welcome them here. The table is set, beautiful platters with barbequed salmon, chunks of lamb stuffed with garlic and rosemary, warm bread, little potatoes drawn from their earthy nest and roasted in olive oil, that salad gathered in early morning. Bowls of raspberries wait, picked from the canes that have only just been planted, cream whipped to soft peaks. I've gathered enough chairs for everyone to sit, taken the summer plates out of their box, painted with figs and dark grapes. The fig tree a seedling, the grapes sending out first tendrils. Wind-chimes are making music of the air and the Supremes sing. There are babies and children and the very old. Time to open the cold wine, fill the glasses all polished and shining. Nighthawks swoop for mosquitoes, quick as sparks in the falling light. The loons are mourning the end of the day.

> You can't hurry love.
> No, you just have to wait,
> You got to trust, give it time.
> No matter how long it takes.[1]

The River Door

A child is life's memory of itself.[1]

IN JUNE, 1917, Dominion Land Surveyor E.S. Martindale compiled a report for the Superintendent of School Lands in Ottawa, providing the names of those squatting on a portion of Sections 10 and 11, Township 29, Range 20, west of the 4th Meridian in Drumheller, Alberta. Each name was accompanied by a description of a house and any outbuildings, their dimensions and location, as well as garden dimensions where applicable. The land, forming a loose community of squatters, was to be subdivided and sold. Those living on the land were to be given an opportunity to buy their individual lots at a public auction. Martindale was also tasked with surveying the land. An earlier set of blueprints detailing a preliminary survey had been submitted by Mr. L.E. Fontaine, D.L.S., the previous June but it was felt that he had not followed the instructions given by the Surveyor General, E. Deville, and Martindale was asked to do the job again.

The correspondence regarding this survey, the sale of lots, and the relationships between various levels of government as well as between bureaucrats and the squatters themselves is a complicated tangle.[2] Eventually, in November 1917, most of the lots were sold (though a number were advertised in the Drumheller Land Company ads in the

Drumheller Mail for a few years after). A list of successful buyers includes some of those who were living in the squatters' community but not all of them. I am particularly interested in Lots 6 and 9 in Block 52, because my grandmother's first husband Joseph Yopek "owned" the house and garden situated on Lot 9 and her brother Joseph Klus "owned" the one on Lot 6. Joseph Yopek's house was 20 feet by 25 feet. It was valued at $150.00. Joseph Klus's house was built into the riverbank and was 10 feet by 15 feet, valued at $25.00.

They lived there, in a community of shacks, dugouts, and holes in the riverbank. Some of them died during the Spanish flu pandemic including Joseph Yopek, and by the time I can find any more information about my grandmother, she was living on the north side of the river with her second husband—my grandfather—and eight children, eventually nine.

We've come to Drumheller on a cold weekend in April with our son, daughter-in-law, and their two young children. We drove from Edmonton in separate cars and John and I arrive first. I am hoping to find some trace of the small farm where my grandparents lived when my father was a child; with a few tattered remnants I am trying to locate the place for my personal archive, on its own map. A place that foresees a woman in the next century with two photographs, no clear sense of how to access survey maps, but a desire to know where things began in this country for her own family. It's for my children and their children as much as for myself. We are hybrids, grafts on branches from several continents, but I know that a body can yearn for the soil of its origins and I want us all to know where that soil might be found. Notes towards a map would help. And for the children, dinosaurs were deeply embedded in the rock and soil of the area, reconstructed in museums and interpreted in strange configurations on the wide Drumheller streetscapes. The children could see close at hand the skeleton of an Albertosaurus and I could trace my finger along the geologic formations in an old photograph, held to the light in what I hoped was its original location.

My grandmother was born in a small village in Moravia, nestled into the Beskydy Mountains. Her first husband came from Poland, which was just a stone's throw away. They married in her village in 1903 and he left twice, once to work in West Virginia, and the second time, in 1912, to Alberta, following in the footsteps of his brother Paul. Anna was pregnant when Joseph left the second time, her fourth pregnancy (the second resulted in twins), and she left her village to join him in Drumheller a year later, travelling first to Antwerp where she boarded the *Mount Temple* and sailed in steerage with her five children, one of them the infant born in Joseph's absence. She arrived to the shack in the squatters' community and by 1917, when the survey was completed, she and Joseph had eight children; a ninth, baby Myrtle, was born the next spring.

Almost everything I know about this period in my grandmother's life, I've learned by reading old documents, parsing one or two family photographs, taking apart stories and looking at each part to learn the truth, or what might be construed as a truth, more than a century later. My father didn't talk much about his early childhood. I knew that the people we called our aunts and uncles were his half sisters and brothers, born to his grandmother and that first husband, Joseph Yopek. I'd been told, or overheard maybe, that he'd had a Dominion homestead grant. A few years ago, I found his name on the Alberta Genealogical Society's Alberta Homestead Index.[3] I noted the numbers defining his section of land and arranged to see the letters patent at the Alberta Archives on a trip to Edmonton. But when I arrived, I was shown instead a microfilm detailing a long saga associated with the land I thought he owned. That my father either believed or never questioned that Joseph had owned. That is the saga of the School Lands in Drumheller, where squatters, deprived of housing by the mines that employed them or for other reasons I am still trying to determine, built shacks and created gardens. One account of life in the community describes the houses:

> "The houses were longer one way than the other, and could be converted into two rooms. They had a caravan roof, had

tar-paper on the outside walls and roof and, as at the Sterling [mine] had no water or toilet inside. Those houses with children had bunkbeds put along the back wall."[4]

In my grandmother's family, there were five children, then six, then seven, then eight. By the time the ninth was born, the auction of the School Lands lots had taken place and the lots Anna and Joseph lived on and had their garden, as well as the nearby lot where Anna's brother, also Joseph, lived, were sold and not to them. Joseph Thompson bought Lot 6, where Joseph Klus had built his shack into the river-bank; and Francis Vint bought Lot 9.

Almost everything I know I've teased out from old documents, a few forlorn images, the 398 digitized pages of PAA Acc. 1970.313, Film 2539, File 31177. But some things remain mysteries. Did my grandmother know Joseph Yopek would not greet her with a home-stead, piles of fence posts to carry wire for acres, a place of their own? Did he tell her immediately, was she shocked, did she unpack her bags in the shack and get to work, making the most of it, her children learning the new ground in a language that marked them? Were there tears and anger?

This was Drumheller around the time when my grandmother met my grandfather and married him. [General view of Drumheller, Alberta, ca. 1920, courtesy of the Glenbow Library and Archive at the University of Calgary, NA-1142-1.]

(The door, if you could see it, would overlook the river,
just west of the town.)

Thirty years ago, my father told me his family had lived near what's now the Royal Tyrrell Museum, near Midland Provincial Park. I filed that information away and sort of forgot it. Until I remembered. I'd been looking at the 1926 census and found my grandparents on it, with the eight surviving children of my grandmother's first marriage (the first child of her second marriage, Julia, born in 1921, died in 1924; and my father's birth was a few months after the census was conducted), in an area described as Township 29 Range 20 West of the 4th Meridian (Rural Parts). And then Midland Road, Michichi. At first I was confused. Michichi is a hamlet some distance from Drumheller, yet I remember a photograph of my father as an altar boy at St. Anthony's Church in Drumheller. Never once did he mention Michichi.

But then, peering closely at a contemporary map of Drumheller, I saw a creek entering the river on its north bank just west of the bridge: Michichi Creek. And the Dinosaur Trail leading to the museum crossed a smaller bridge over the creek, following the route of what had once been Midland Road. You could walk this distance if you were a person without a car (my grandmother) taking your chickens and eggs to market to barter for flour and sugar or to sell to the mines. You could ride this distance if you were a boy with a bike (my father) heading to town for the parade or on errands for your mother or to St. Anthony's Church on Sunday.

"The date was October 2, 1918. The terrible Spanish influenza was sweeping the world, leaving millions dead. A week earlier I had been teaching school in the small town of Carmangay in southern Alberta. Now all schools were closed. Besides my teacher's certificate, I held certificates in first aid, home nursing and motor mechanics. These qualified me as a member of the Voluntary Aid Detachment."[5]

I'm not used to using the grid or checkerboard survey developed by the Canadian government to organize the Prairies to find a place on a map—the townships, the sections, the various meridians. And to be honest? I saw those numbers on the census but they didn't register. Not in the way "Midland Road" did, precipitating the recovery of the memory of my father's reply when I asked him where his family had lived when he was a child: "If you drove to the Tyrrell Museum, did you notice the Midland Mine day-use area with the old mine office and the trail? Near there." Anything he ever told me about the past, about his childhood, about his family was terse, evasive. Did your parents have brothers or sisters? "Never asked." And so on. Yet his answer to my question about location was uncharacteristically detailed. My memory is my compass as I think about roads and what they bisect, how the verbs have their faded conjugations: homesteads with collapsed fences, letters patent written in faded ink and crumbling in file folders, chickens ruffling their feathers in the dust.

(And yet, the hell holes were homes.)

"'Drumheller was hit worse than others, partly because the living conditions were terrible. This was an era where Drumheller was called Hell's Hole because the living conditions were so terrible. Primitive shacks, latrines which were never cleaned and latrines which were too close to the water supply,' says the Atlas Coal Mine's Linda Digby. 'This was when the population explosion had just happened and the infrastructure just wasn't there.'"[6]

I thought perhaps they'd bought other lots in the School Lands area and stayed on for a time and maybe I'd somehow missed seeing their names on the list of successful bids. Then I read this, in an announcement of the auction and others, published in the nearby Hanna newspaper:

> "Any person who was not, at the commencement of the present war, and who has not since continued to be a British subject, or a subject or a citizen of a country which is an ally of his Majesty in the present war, or a subject of a neutral country, is prohibited from purchasing any of these lands under penalty of having the sales cancelled and the payments made thereon forfeited."[7]

I might have known this. Should have known this. I think of all the Central and Eastern Europeans (and others of course but this is where mine came from; these are the stories I know) brought to Canada by companies like the North Atlantic Trading Company, contracted by Clifford Sifton (Minister of the Interior), and the CPR, who advertised that they could help arrange tickets, affidavits, and other legal considerations. Brought, and then what? Those who didn't or couldn't receive Dominion homestead grants, but who were needed as labour in mines? In a local history written about Drumheller, with individual families adding their stories, someone remembers Mrs. Cattini: "She lived in a tent for four years, cooking outside on a big cookstove. She had to haul her water for drinking, cooking, and washing for two miles on a stoneboat. They had ten children, eight of them died in the flu of 1918."[8]

A woman named Mrs. Bond tells of how rudimentary housing was provided by the mines if a family was lucky but then when the mines laid off workers, those families were homeless. Mrs. Bond's husband cobbled together a house on the School Lands; it's her description of the houses around them that I quote earlier and it's her descriptions of family life during those years that helps me to imagine my own grandmother in her shack on the Red Deer River. When Mrs. Bond's husband enlisted in the army and was away, in winter, she wrote of having to pack her water from the river in a tub on a sleigh.

> "We had to let the pail down by pulley to a hole in the ice. If you didn't go for water when the hole in the ice was open, you had to go down and break the hole open yourself. Two tubs filled our water barrel. We generally boiled water for drinking and cooking."[9]

Mrs. Bond had three children. My grandmother had eight, then nine. How many trips to the hole in the ice in winter? One woman, Mrs. Michielin,[10] died of typhoid fever after drinking water from the Red Deer River where she'd been washing her family's laundry, as she'd washed laundry in rivers as a girl growing up in Italy. She was too shy to go to the new hospital, built in the aftermath of the flu pandemic, and died on the earth floor of her shack.

My father in his little car, ca. 1929.

We have a little time before meeting Brendan, Cristen, and
our grandchildren so we cross to the north bank of the Red Deer
River, drive over the Michichi Creek bridge, and head along the
Dinosaur Trail to see if we can find a place that somehow matches the
landscape in the two photographs I have of my father's early home.

There is a modest subdivision between the road and the
river and then more houses on the north side of the Dinosaur Trail.
We drive to where the houses ended north of the road and get out
of our car. Looking southeast, towards the Red Deer River, we can
almost imagine we are seeing what could be determined beyond the
small boy (my father) riding towards us on a tricycle, a dog behind
him watching the road. We can see the far banks of the river, the trees
(aspens, balsam poplars, cottonwoods, willows near the banks, and

My father on his tricycle, ca. 1930.

are those elms, I wonder, with their tiny new leaves?) softening the view. Breathe, breathe in, as though the scent of dry cold earth can tell me something. Anything.

I point my camera towards the hills beyond the houses. The view feels familiar somehow.

Hinge

1. n. Movable joint or mechanism like that by which door is hung on side post; natural joint doing similar work...; (fig.) central principle, critical point, on which all turns.
2. v.t. Attach (as) with[11]

In these days of the latest pandemic, when we are told not to leave our houses unless absolutely necessary, to wear masks, to avoid all social contact, I go through the old documents, the old photographs. I read the issues of the Drumheller newspaper as it reported the Spanish flu outbreak:

"Spanish Influenza, which is sweeping through the States and eastern Canada has arrived at Calgary. Six cases were reported there on Wednesday morning having been brought into the city by returned soldiers from Montreal. Four cases were taken from the train at a point in Saskatchewan. Dr. Mahood of Calgary gave out the following statement:

It is well for the citizens to learn something of the disease and how to avoid it. The onset is sudden and individuals may be attacked on the street or while at work. Symptoms consist of sudden chill, headache, elevation of temperature, pains in various parts of the body, sore throat, herpes on lips and prostration, followed in many cases by pneumonia. It is important that affected individuals go home and to bed at once and place themselves under a physician's care and should remain in bed until all symptoms disappear. Special care should be exercised during convalescence to avoid the serious complication, pneumonia."[12]

A few weeks later:

"The greater number of deaths were cases brought in from the mines where there was no way of giving the patients proper care in the early stages of the disease."[13]

"Care of masks: Have several. Change them frequently. Boil 20 minutes before using again. If removed for a few minutes for any reason care should be taken that the side that was next the face is again next the face. It is not necessary to use any antiseptic on the mask when in use.

Several parties have been checked up this week by the authorities for not wearing masks while on the streets. This is a provincial order."[14]

Are these the same hills in the photograph of my father in his little car?

Behind the sheds and the boy racing in a metal car, are those the same hills?

I snap again.

Imagine the small farm tucked against the flank of hill. Imagine waking to the striations, walking out to the morning in the shadow of those layers to scatter grain for the chickens, throw a precious handful of hay to the cow. This was his whole world until he moved to live with a sister in Beverly and then joined the navy for a life at sea. My father once wrote a letter to me when I was living in Ireland, so it must have been 1978, and he mentioned he'd been to the funeral of his last living (half) brother, Paul Yopek. He'd driven to Drumheller after that funeral and wrote that he saw the hills where he'd walked as a boy but had never found anything worth keeping

Were we more or less in the same place where my father raced his little trike while his dog watched the road behind him?

in his life. I thought he meant fossils but perhaps his comment was more ontological. Looking at the sedimentary layers exposed by weather, the mudstone, sandstone, the coal seams, and shale, all softly coloured and shimmering in the light, I wondered if they might take up a large space in the metaphysical topography of a boy growing in their shadows. Paleontologists were at work in the 1930s when my father was a boy and perhaps he encountered one on his forays into the hills. Maybe he'd been asked to keep his eyes open. Maybe he had and nothing ever showed up. The long rib of a creature as old as time. An ammonite. A nest of fossilized eggs. In his rough house, his mother made noodles, his father came home dark with coal dust.

The announcement about the auctions on the School Lands said that current occupants would "be allowed until the first of June, 1918 to remove any improvements they may have on the land."[14] So this takes us forward, forward, the spring surge of the river after breakup, rising waters, the poplars greening: Mrs. Bond remembered, "the Gumbo was very bad on the roads here when it rained and we always struck across the field to the railroad track during wet weather, otherwise you would lose your footwear in the gumbo."[16]

They had a winter and then a spring—where? Whatever happened in the winter and spring, my grandmother was pregnant. My grandmother's ninth child, Myrtle, was born on July 1, 1918. Was there a garden that year? A cow? When their lot was sold to Francis Vint, did they leave immediately, carting their house on a wagon across the river or were arrangements made for them to stay in place? This takes us forward, forward, but to where? To the other side of the river but when?

In May and June of 1918, when the Spanish flu arrived in Canada—where were they living then?

"'They need help desperately at Drumheller,' she said. 'The flu seems to have taken a particularly virulent form among the miners. They even believe it's the Black Death of Medieval Europe all over again. There's no hospital but the town council has taken over the new' [sic] school to house the sick.'"[17]

Where were they living when the flu arrived? I see them, mid-river, a wagon of their belongings, paused. Paused between homes, between what they'd known and what was to come, the moment a hinge on the river door.

The funeral of my father's sister Julia Kishkan, 1924.

A big dog barks behind a fence in the last house as we walk the edge of the road, wondering about the individual pleats in the hills. Would the homestead have been there, or there? Or there? Parked by the house, a big Dodge Ram pickup truck, detailed with polished chrome and with plush dice hanging from the rear-view mirror, had a sign painted on its side, in big decorative lettering: Canadians Against the Temporary Foreign Workers Program.

And was this the house? On the back of the photograph: *The old house at Drumheller, Julia's funeral.* Julia, born in 1921, dead of septic tonsillitis at the age of three. My grandfather, still a foreign worker.

"Rumour had it that the men from Ivankivtsi had begun to emigrate to Canada around 1908–09 after Hnat Pychko, one of the village residents, met a mysterious 'American entrepreneur' during his sojourn in Odessa—a major seasonal destination for Ivankivtsi peasants. Soon after the fateful meeting Hnat set out on a journey to Canada, where he bought some land 'in the city of Saskaton' [sic], 'started a business,' and eventually sent for his wife and four children. Over the course of several years about half of the Ivankivtsi population caught the emigration fever, leaving behind mostly children, elders, and women."[18]

My grandmother, a foreigner, her name and nationality fluid on the papers that described her over her decades in Canada. She is Bohemian, Polish, Moravian, Silesian, Austro-Hungarian, German, she is Anna, she is Annie, she is Anne, she is a mother eight times, nine times, ten times, eleven. A sister, a widow, a wife (again).

"But when the workers arrived, they discovered overcrowded canvas tents infested with bedbugs. There were no medical facilities or clean drinking water, and diseases like typhoid spread like a prairie fire. The bosses grouped immigrant workers who spoke different languages on the same work teams to prevent them from organizing. Living conditions in the valley were so bad that soldiers returning from the First World War began calling Drumheller the 'Western Front,' claiming that conditions in the valley's mining towns were worse than those in the trenches."[19]

"...seek to make nature your ally."[20]

The first time someone knocked on our door since the pandemic began, I felt my heart race. I couldn't move. You'll have to go, I told my husband. He did, and it was a neighbour, bringing some of our mail that had ended up in his box. He put it on the post at the top of the stairs so that no one had to come out. Hearing his voice, I came to say hello through the screen door. He stood well back. After he left, I opened the door. For several weeks no one but us had stood on the other side, looking in; or on our deck, looking out at the world. My company had been my husband, and the dead who stood around me at night.

Daily we learn new things about how to behave, what to avoid. I read obsessively, looking for clues about how people living in shacks on the banks of a river a hundred years ago might have tried to save themselves.

"1. Avoid needless crowding—influenza is a crowd disease.
2. Smother your coughs and sneezes—others do not want the germs which you would throw away. 3. Your nose, not your mouth was made to breathe through—get the habit.
4. Remember the three C's—a clean mouth, clean skin, and clean clothes. 5. Try to keep cool when you walk and warm when you ride and sleep. 6. Open the windows—always at home at night; at the office when practicable. 7. Food will win the war if you give it a chance—help by choosing and chewing your food well. 8. Your fate may be in your own hands—wash your hands before eating. 9. Don't let the waste products of digestion accumulate—drink a glass or two of water on getting up.
10. Don't use a napkin, towel, spoon, fork, glass or cup which has been used by another person and not washed. 11. Avoid tight clothes, tight shoes, tight gloves—seek to make nature your ally not your prisoner. 12. When the air is pure breathe all of it you can—breathe deeply. GEORGE A. SOPER, SANITARY CORPS, U.S.A."[21]

I didn't know what to do next. Did it matter if I knew, or didn't know, where my father was a child, where he raced across bare ground on a tricycle, where he left each day for school, accompanied to the grade one classroom for a time by his mother who eased her large body into a small chair and tried to learn to read alongside her son. Where was that school? Did it matter now, did it ever, and why didn't I ask when my father could have taken down a map of Drumheller and shown me exactly where to look. If he had such a map. If he was willing to talk.

Did it matter? Somehow it did.

In Ottawa a couple of weeks later, my older son Forrest, familiar not only with archival resources but also with fancy systems to view them online, asks for copies of the photographs I have—the ones of my father on his trike and little car and the ones we took in Drumheller on the last weekend in April. He turns them, zooms in, then out, takes a small detail and expands it to look at the line of a hill across the sky. "I think you're in the right location," he says. "Look here, and here, and here." He finds a street view of the very place we'd walked around in cold air and swirls it around on his computer screen. He angles closer to the hills, the peculiar cone-shaped one, and around it. My husband, who was with me when we walked behind the last houses above the Dinosaur Trail, tells him again of how the Red Deer River and its opposite shore looked from where we stood, and reminds me of what we could see and what we couldn't. Forrest uses some mapping program and figures out from the details on the 1926 census, the details I'd skimmed over, where exactly on the Midland Road the enumerator questioned my grandparents about their first language (which he or she got wrong), the place they came from (wrong again, in my grandmother's case), the names of the children my grandmother brought into the marriage in 1920 (and again, one of the names was incorrect). The only person on record to have owned the land was James Edward Trumble. Did my grandparents buy a small piece from him? He'd taken out the first coal lease in the valley, in 1901. Forrest finds them on the 1921 census. I'd looked and couldn't find a match but he used alternate spellings of my grandfather's surname (my surname) and sure enough, yes. There it was, missing significant letters, but the roll call of stepchildren trailing after his name and my grandmother's. A section was listed this time, Section 11.

The paper trail from 1915 to 1918 asserts that the squatters were living on the N E and S W quarters of Section 11 and the S E quarter of Section 10. And this was the land that was subdivided, or at least some of it was. The N W sections must have been across the river but I haven't been able to determine that with any certainty. I've written to librarians and genealogy sites and the information given is contradictory in some ways but then when I read more closely and do some basic math, I realize that in one case the researcher is looking at the 1921 census information for Joseph Yopek's brother Paul, who seems to have children with similar names to the ones born to my grandmother and Joseph Yopek. Someone else believes the property I have in mind was the hamlet of Nacmine, three miles west of the centre of Drumheller and now part of the town proper. One librarian demurred when I asked about the squatters' community. She thought there might have been temporary settlements east of town but certainly not where I suggested it might have been, certainly nothing so established as what E.S. Martindale's reports had enumerated. Two women in the Visitor Centre looked at the fragment of map I'd copied, with the small plots laid out, and a bridge straddling the river, and one of them said, "You know, I think that was right here, right where this Visitor Centre is! Because that's the old bridge!" The other woman concurred. And I looked around to make a mental note of where I was: on 1st Avenue West, under the World's Largest Dinosaur, that my grandchildren would embrace and be photographed leaning against. I thought of the area dense with rough shacks, subsistence gardens, the smoke of their fires hanging in the air. The voices of their children, their dogs, an unruly rooster. And surely most of them were people who had dreamed of land, had come to the area hoping for a homestead grant, the prospect of creating a place of their own.

("Any person who was not, at the commencement of the
present war, and who has not since continued to be a
British subject, or a subject or a citizen of a country which
is an ally of his Majesty in the present war, or a subject of a
neutral country, is prohibited from purchasing any of these
lands under penalty of having the sales cancelled and the
payments made thereon forfeited."[22])

Potential settlers, following a dream that ended for some in shacks
or shelters built underground or in the side of the riverbank, ended
in Spanish influenza or failure. Followed a few years later by a short
migration across the bridge to barren land near Michichi Creek.

"Eighty men tossed feverishly on their low beds. Even as a man was dying, another was waiting to occupy his bed. A man often died alone, among strangers who could not understand him even when he was only begging for water. Terror of the Black Death kept family or friends from visiting him. Some victims never even got to our hospital; they had been abandoned to die alone in a dugout or shack."[23]

I look, and look again. Was it here the washtubs were stored, in full view of the singular hill, layered with history as my thinking is layered? Was that the river beyond the cottonwoods, the road with its little haze of dust? Yearning is a cloudy overlay. As much as I want to see the thing clear and definite, the land, the house, the road leading to town, and away to the places my father walked, looking for bones, I am lost in the contours of paper and dirt. My thumb rasps old paper. Wandering down the gravel road alongside the barren ground with its tufts of tough grass, broken bottles at the edge, a few brave grasshoppers clicking, I keep my face averted from the truck with the Canadians Against the Temporary Foreign Workers Program sign. I will it away. Away. On the map I can't draw or annotate but keep clear in my imagination, I can find the exact location where my Canadian family (all foreign workers, domestic, miners, subsistence farmers) began. The cone-shaped hill holds more than its layers of mudstone, sandstone, shales, and seams of dark coal. Within the hill, the fossilized bodies of dinosaurs large and small, later mammals, reptiles, fish, trees as unlikely as giant redwoods and mulberries in that dry land. On its steep slope, my father lingers. My finger traces the road, the place where Michichi Creek enters the Red Deer River, its elbows of ice, and the pike and walleye resting in the shadows. I smell the mineral scent of the waters, far away rain in the clouds. My father is riding towards me, hell-bent for town. He is three. He is thirteen. He is a man bent by the news that his brother died.

"Sixteen of the most seriously ill patients were moved into one ward and these became my charge. In their delirium they reverted to their own languages. Many seemed obsessed with the idea of running away and had to be strapped to their beds."[24]

I find the names of Joseph Yopek and Joseph Klus in the lists of the dead:

"Klus—At Drumheller, Oct. 26 1918, Joseph A. Klus, Austrian, aged 41 years.
Yopek—At Drumheller, Oct. 28, 1918, Joseph Yopek, German. aged 40 yrs."[25]

Among the others in this list, a man who is described, in brackets, as "coloured," several infants, a couple of young children (one of them described as "colored"), and many men of early to middle age.

Early on the morning we are to leave Drumheller, I open the door of the little house we are staying in. My grandchildren are playing with puzzles, their parents and my husband are making breakfast. I walk to the river, just a block or two away. The trail is crisp with frost and the willows hang over quiet eddies of the dark water. Was it here? One map suggests it was. Was this where Joseph Klus dug his house into the bank, laid his blankets on a cot, listened for rain? Is this where he first felt the chill, the congestion in his lungs, shivered until he was moved to his sister's house where he died among the children, one of them an infant? Did anyone bring soup or tubs of water for washing his body? Two days later, Joseph Yopek also died, in Anna's care.

Was it here or was it across the river? Magpies watch me walking. There's a hotel I've seen in early photographs and someone told me the squatters' camp was in that area. Our little house looks out on the hotel. Was it here, was it here? Everyone is nice to me but I know they don't understand my urgent need to determine where my grandmother lived, where she lost first one, then a second, and finally a third family member in a short period of time. Baby Myrtle died of whooping cough with the underlying condition of malnutrition. I can't imagine my grandmother took to her bed, not with nine children, but did her milk dry up as she grieved her losses, in a place without its language, without her extended family? Was there no money to supplement the infant's diet?

Was it here, where the children were sent for water, were hushed while both Josephs coughed themselves to death? Was it here the coal smoke rose from their chimney, carrying the souls to heaven?

There were doors, small openings. The slag heaps where people collected enough coal to heat their shacks. Coal seams ran under some of the houses and people could hear the picks below ground as they hung out laundry, fed their chickens. A door opens, someone is sweeping an earth floor, sweeping the crumbs out to the chickens, unpegging the sheets and diapers from the line. A few mended shirts are draped over bushes, their empty sleeves spread wide.

In our own pandemic, over a hundred years later, I can't separate their story from my own. It is my own, a century ago. When I wake in the night, they are standing in my room, quietly, waiting for me to come downstairs and resume writing. I am writing them into a history that has forgotten them, apart from a few names on graves, the handful of forms listing deaths, a marriage, the transfer of citizenship from one country to another, one continent a lifetime ago to this one.

But *where* precisely was the squatters' camp where they lived? I want to know, in time and in space. Requests to town planners for information go unanswered. In the digital version of the microfilm I was sent by my son in 2016, after I'd discovered the information about the camp and their residence there, I can see tattered pieces of a map but some are missing and I can't make any sense of it.

Online, I search. I send queries and most go out into space and never return. But then one does. A librarian at the University of Calgary, responding to my query about maps of early Drumheller, locates several in the holdings the library acquired from the Glenbow Museum. But we were in the early stages of the COVID-19 pandemic and he said that the maps were inaccessible for the time being. I went through his list and realized that one of the maps was the original of the very one in tatters on the digital file.

I'd followed the process of the subdividing of the School Lands in the file, from discussions about how much land should be considered—

> "I find that a considerable portion of the 11.4 acres has been washed away by the waters of the Red Deer River and that a number of the squatters' shacks have been carried away down the river for miles..."[26]

—to ruminations about valuing the shacks of those who lived on the lands ("I beg to point out that on some of the acres there will be from 4–8 shacks...") and the best way to effect the transfer to the land (the School Lands Section 11) to Drumheller, with some subtextual murmurings, re: legality:

"The difficulty is that there is, apparently, no authority under the Dominion Lands' Act for an exchange of this nature, so that it is at least doubtful whether a transfer of this parcel to the Town would be legal. I don't suppose, however, that if it were made anyone would question it, especially if we obtained an Order-In-Council from the Provincial Government concurring, but the title of the Town would be doubtful."[27]

E.S. Martindale was assigned to the job of surveying the proposed subdivision into lots to be sold at public auction. His work was delayed.

"Referring to your memorandum of the 31st of March, file 31177 School Lands herewith, the subdividing of the lots in Sections 10 and 11, Township 20-20-4, has not yet been completed. Mr. E.S. Martindale, D.L.S., who last year laid out a number of the lots in the above Sections was unable to plant the townsite posts at the lot corners on account of the frozen ground."[28]

But then it was complete and the map shows up in the correspondence as received:

"I beg to enclose you, herewith, a blue print of the plan of the survey of the Subdivision of a portion of Sections 10 and 11, Township 29, Range 20, West of the 4th Meridian, adjoining the Town of Drumheller, and would request that you have authorities kindly examine this blue print and notify the Department if the Subdivision is now satisfactory to the Town."[29]

A hundred and three years later, I look at the map with wonder and with recognition.

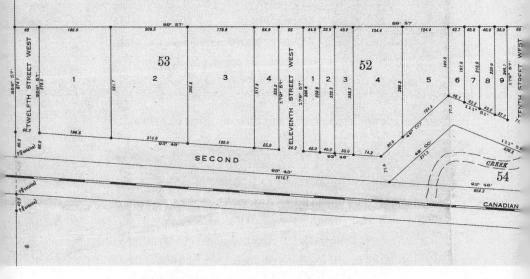

PLAN OF
Red Deer Addition to
DRUMHELLER

Being parts of the southeast quarter of Section 10 and
the southwest quarter of Section 11, Township 29,
Range 20, West of Fourth Meridian

PROVINCE OF ALBERTA

Scale : 200 feet to an inch.

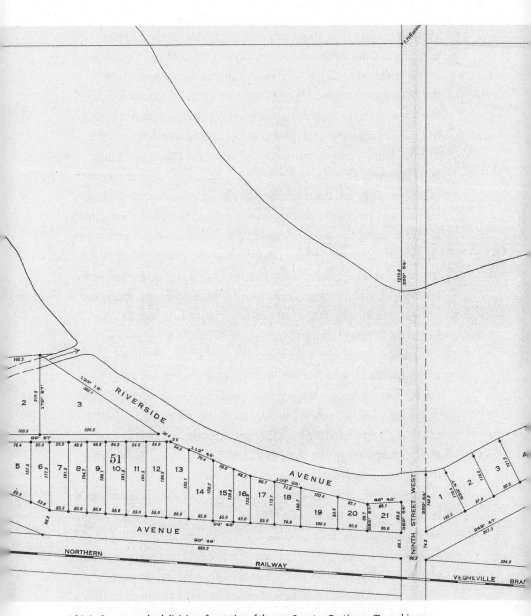

This is the proposed subdivision of a portion of the S W Quarter, Section 11, Township 29,
Range 20, West of the 4th Meridian, drawn by E.S. Martindale in 1917.

[S.L. Evans, L.E. Fontaine, E.S. Martindale, and Canada Surveyor General's Office. Plan of Red
Deer Addition to Drumheller, Being Parts of the Southeast Quarter of Section 10 and the Southwest
Quarter of Section 11, Township 29, Range 20, West of Fourth Meridian, Province of Alberta. Ottawa:
Department of the Interior, 1917. Print. Courtesy of Glenbow Map Collection, University of Calgary
Archives and Special Collections.]

There is the Red Deer River, its gentle arm where I walked that
morning in Drumheller while my husband, my son, and my daughter-
in-law prepared breakfast while my grandchildren played in the
little house we'd rented. I opened the door of the little house on the
Newcastle Trail and walked to the river. Was it here or was it across
the river? Magpies watched me walking. I compared the map with
a contemporary one of Drumheller, showing the Newcastle Trail,
Riverside Avenue W, and the creek running down the river adjacent
to Newcastle Beach Recreation Area. The little house was two blocks
from where my grandmother and her husband had lived, their garden
along the creek. I opened the door that morning and walked where my
aunts as children might have played, where my grandmother might
have chased her chickens, traded homemade butter with a neighbour
for some needed foodstuff or cloth for children's clothing, where my
uncles as small boys might have constructed rafts in the shallows,
fished for a Friday supper.

I knew something that morning as I walked. The scent of the river
reminded me of my father's memories of swimming, his walks to
school over the bridge, his own small, hoarded stories of rafts and
drownings. Did he know it was here where his mother arrived after
travelling by boat and train such a distance, one continent to another,
one language to another, from a plum orchard to a squatters' settlement, more babies to feed, not enough money.

A year later, sheltered at home for the past four and a half months
because of the pandemic, I think of the creek running through the plot
where my grandmother grew her vegetables, and wonder how she
managed to cope when her husband died. When I return home from
a careful trip to buy groceries, I immediately wash my mask.

Small boys might have constructed rafts in the shallows, as my
father did on the north side, using old boards, fence posts washed from
fields during flooding, maybe even a door—*I find that a considerable
portion of the 11.4 acres has been washed away by the waters of the Red
Deer River and that a number of the squatters' shacks have been carried
away down the river for miles*—drifting on slow water as Huckleberry
Finn did in the story my father loved, where the boys find an entire

house floating on the river, the House of Death, and as William Dawe did in *Badlands*, taking to the river in search of dinosaur bones two years before the Spanish flu arrived in Drumheller, ten years before my father was born.

Somewhere I read that sick men were taken from shacks on doors removed from their hinges, walked over rough ground to the road where a vehicle could take them to the rudimentary medical facilities. I think of Joseph Klus, unmarried, living in a shelter created in the riverbank. And was he carried away on his own door, a few rough boards hammered together, carried away to his final home in the Drumheller Cemetery? He has no stone, no marker. He is almost forgotten.

We are unhinging your door, Joseph Klus. (Careful as you lift him. No one a hundred years from now will remember his birthdate, his house in the riverbank, door opening to water and light, his unshaven face, bedding his sister will wash with the sheets from the bed where her husband lies, coughing and chilled. She will wash sheets and hang them out in autumn air, wondering what will come of her and the nine children waiting to be fed. In the village where he was born, no one remembers him.) We are unhinging your door and you will enter your next earthen home among strangers in a strange land, your name in the newspaper your small cryptic epitaph.

The Starland Fonds

"The fonds consists of minutes, bylaws, seed grain registers, cash disbursement and receipt books, assessment and tax rolls, of the following former local authorities of Starland County dating from 1910 to 1943: Local Improvement District 15-P-4, Local Improvement District 15-N-4, Local Improvement District No. 277, the Municipal District of Starland No. 307, the Municipal District of Lambton No. 306, and the Municipal District of Michichi No. 277. The fonds also includes two maps illustrating land boundaries for Starland County."[30]

My older son, a historian and archivist, suggested looking at the Starland County Fonds: three reels of microfilm, and two maps. Unlike the digital version of the microfilm detailing the dissolution of the squatters' settlement where my family began their residence in Canada more than a century earlier, these reels are only available to read on screen in the Provincial Archives of Alberta in Edmonton. During the pandemic, I've thought of that room often, the room where I first learned of the settlement, found my grandmother's first husband's name on petitions and lists, and from where I came away, driving to Drumheller with my husband to see if I might be able to figure out how to find traces of the life they lived before Joseph Yopek died, leaving my grandmother a widow. In the afternoons I listen to my province's medical health officer list the new cases of our particular virus, the deaths, and I wash my masks, plan my single weekly shopping trip.

Two trips to Drumheller resulted in a little more information but not the location of the settlement (though that arrived in the form of a map, elegantly drawn on paper now yellowed with age), nor the confirmed location of the second home my grandmother made with her new husband, though by using old photographs and new ones, I think I know which fold in the hill near Michichi Creek held the rough house, the galvanized wash tub, the small boy racing across the dust on his tricycle, his metal car. One day I will visit the PAA and sit down to view the Starland Fonds to see if I can determine whether my family owned their land on the north side of the Red Deer River or if they leased or even if they were squatters on what seems to be the quarter section owned by James Edward Trumble.

Somehow they crossed the river with all their worldly goods, my grandmother and eight or nine children, because I don't know if this was before Myrtle's death, or after. Before her marriage to my grandfather, or after. I may never know how, nor when. I have a photograph of them in 1924 in front of a plain board house, with a solemn crowd there for the funeral of Julia Kishkan, my father's only full sister, the firstborn of my grandmother and her second husband. A chicken saunters in front of the children, the men in their jackets, my grandmother with her sad face, my grandfather beside her, his shirt buttoned up to his throat. They have survived the pandemic, only to lose Julia to septicaemia caused by tonsillitis. She is in the satin-lined coffin, ready to join her half sister Myrtle in the Drumheller Cemetery. Sisters, says their tombstone. Sisters, who never met, the younger who never would have been if not for the death of Joseph Yopek and the journey through the old door of the shack in the squatters' settlement. A door opens, a door closes, the river surges not far away, and in the future I am looking for them, hoping to find them, the embodiment of the shadows who have entered my room as I wait out another version of what changed their lives.

I don't need the seed grain registers or bylaws but only the evidence of my family on land I have seen, under hills as grey and layered as time. In this pandemic that is an echo of their own, I have learned a patience that keeps me awake in the night, hoping for their company.

Museum of the Multitude Village

This is the greatest consolation in life. In poetically well-built museums, formed from the heart's compulsions, we are consoled not by finding in them old objects that we love, but by losing all sense of Time.[1]

Exhibit 1 | small museums

I was doing what I often do: Googling my surname to try to find any links to my paternal grandfather who immigrated to North America in 1907 and who had one living child, my father. When my father died in 2009, I took home the little chocolate box, labelled Moirs Happiness Package, with the meagre hoard of papers associated with his parents. I came to know a little more about his mother, Anna Klusova, who came to Canada in 1913 to join her first husband. I've written about her and have also visited her birthplace in what's now the Czech Republic. But my grandfather was more of a mystery. Did he have brothers and sisters, I wondered when I was a child. I never asked him, was my father's reply. Though he did know of a cousin, in Prince Albert. In later years, my father talked a little to my older son about his father, Forrest's great-grandfather, but none of what he said was precise.

So I Googled and tried to puzzle through what I found. Mostly it was myself I found, and that wasn't interesting because I know the things I was told (how many books, details of education, personal life), but one day it was this, from a site devoted to Ukrainian places of interest. The piece was titled "Museum of the Multitude Village," written (or translated) in the most charming way. Reading it, I was surprised to find the surname I shared with my grandfather.

> The museum is located in 4 rooms on the second floor administrative building in the village center. The first room will tell you about the history of the most ancient settlements in the territory multitude, archaeological expeditions in the area. After going to the next room, you will learn the ethnography of edge, things of life of local people, their customs. A special corner of the exhibition dedicated to the history of the local church building (1778). Be sure to attract your attention the ancient Gospel 1764, ancient icons, church supplies. The third exhibition hall tells visitors about the time of World and participation of the villagers multitude. The last exhibition hall housed in the memory of the writer Vasily Kishkan, which also was the founding director of the museum and the local school.[2]

How far was this village, Valyava, from Ivankivtsi, my grandfather's village? Fifteen kilometres. Was this a great distance in 1907, when my grandfather set out for North America, or before, when he either had brothers or didn't, or cousins, who could be visited by horse and wagon? Was it a great distance now?

They are like stars, the appearances of my name, attached to others, lighting the blank space on my computer screen. Like small habitations, seen from a great distance. Some dark nights, at my desk, they seem close enough to touch, one leading to another until there are enough to tell a story.

Exhibit 2 | *Ukrainian Cultural Heritage Village, east of Edmonton*

> On the crest of the hill is the rye, cut high on its blooming stem:
> Down below is a well where the horses drink water drawn
> for them.[3]

You were walking just beyond the pigsty, beyond the wide shorn fields with stooks of hay standing like men waiting for winter, you were pushing the stroller with your baby granddaughter, walking with your husband and son (the baby's father), when a wagon drawn by two horses turned onto the narrow road. Would you like a ride, asked the woman sitting on a bale of straw, scarf tied neatly under her chin, and an apron over her skirt and rough cotton blouse. Of course you wanted a ride. The horses stood quietly while, between the three of you, you hoisted the stroller onto the wagon, and then you climbed on too. Where do you come from, asked the woman, and you knew the rules at this living museum: she was in character, a Ukrainian immigrant from the 1930s, and she would act and talk as though the years between then and now hadn't yet occurred. Ivankivtsi, you replied. And then she whispered, Have you been there yourself? And you whispered back, No, no, I don't even know how to begin to find it. Cobblestone Freeway, she said in a low voice, a woman passing on information best told in secret. Then she was herself again, joshing with the driver, talking about the harvest. You'd been to the Grekul house and wondered if it was somehow like the house your grandfather had grown up in. The big garden was mostly dug over but patches of dill flourished on the perimeter. Chickens pecked over the furrows where beets had already been harvested, the long rows of potatoes waiting for the fork. In the Orthodox church, you crossed yourself entering and leaving.

Weeks later, you remembered what the woman had whispered as the wagon rumbled beneath you on the rough road, the scent of dry straw heady, and you sought out the Cobblestone Freeway team, who made it possible for you to travel to Ukraine, a few years later, in early autumn.

Exhibit 3 | *villages viewed from train windows*

> Impossible now to think of train travel without a kind of
> tenderness—as if that is what love is: arrival after arrival.[4]

I kept pulling aside the little blind over the window at the foot of my
bed on the train from Kyiv to Chernivtsi. It was dark but there were
lights in the little villages we passed: lamplight, streetlights, a few
dim platform lights smudging the edges of the tracks. We'd had cherry
liquor earlier in the evening, a mellow way to pass the hours in a
narrow compartment, talking with our Ukrainian host, an employee
of Cobblestone Freeway, and sharing some chocolate, and then I put
on my cotton nightdress and tried to find the most comfortable position on my side of the compartment. Already our beds had been made
up with a crisp sheet, another folded on top, and two square pillows,
with fresh white cases.

Three times in my life I've spent a night in a train compartment.
No, four, because I traveled from Spain to Brindisi on a train, two
trains (because I changed in Rome), sitting upright with passengers
on either side, and didn't sleep a wink. Around me people drank wine,
smoked, talked all night, eating bread with sliced garlic. I was so
entranced by everything I saw—sleeping villages, a floodlit castle
on a hill, horses racing along some dunes in the southwest of France
as the light returned—that I didn't mind being awake. But the first
time I had a bed on a train was a dreadful experience, travelling from
Bologna to Paris. John and I thought we had a private couchette but
found ourselves instead with four fellow bedmates, amiable young
Italian men heading to a religious gathering. Two of them had heavy
colds and they coughed and sneezed repeatedly, but happily joined
the others for prayers and hymns. I climbed into the top bunk and
tried to get comfortable, knowing I would have to climb down to pee
at least once in the night. It was November. Again, I didn't sleep.
At dawn our train broke down somewhere in central France, just
beyond a village tucked in the bottom of a hill. There was no heat.

The compartment became foggy with condensation. The single toilet on our car backed up. I will never do this again, I said tersely to John, watching the young men say their rosaries while coughing into the shared air, because by then the full quartet was sick. We went outside to stand in the cold on the edge of fields and waited. Eventually a new engine arrived and we proceeded to Paris, late and chilled, with the beginnings of an illness that lasted for weeks.

The second time, a year later, was wonderful. John was trying to get us from the Czech Republic to the Netherlands in the least disruptive way. I'd been sick while in Brno and was recovering slowly. Rather than face the cattle call of one of the cheap airlines taking people from one place to another with the least amount of comfort, he discovered that we had enough points for a first-class overnight train ride from Prague to Amsterdam, the cost minimal. It was memorable. We were greeted with a glass of champagne as we boarded the train. Our couchette had its own tiny bathroom, with a sink that swiveled on a bronze arm, and a shower. Big plush towels. Our beds were made up with fresh white linen. That night I slept so well, awakened only by the sound of the train stopping at stations; when I'd peek through the blind at the end of my bed, I'd see a sign saying Köln or Dresden. A few people on dark platforms, their suitcases beside them and the sound of outer coach doors opening, closing, while I was warm under the duvet. Our porter brought us a breakfast tray of good coffee, croissants, cheese and ham, and glasses of cold orange juice. From the window I watched children in a small village walking to school, someone mopping the entrance to a bar, and smoke rising from chimneys while a slow river ran under a bridge where a man dangled a fishing line and didn't look up at the train.

On the train from Kyiv to Chernivtsi, I saw villages lit with old lamps, I saw them close, and in the distance. And oh, Orion stretched across the sky above one small village, close enough to touch. When I checked my husband's watch, it was 4:30 a.m. I made a little drawing in my notebook, wanting to remember the exact placement of the stars. I was on the train, drawing Orion, and 32,000 years ago, someone in a cave in the Swabian Jura was carving Orion into a length of mammoth bone to make a star map to keep the memory of a constellation at hand. I could almost hear the cows lowing in the fields to be milked, to be given a handful of hay from the stooks that stood close to the houses. The train took us from darkness to light and from the present to a place where my own ancestors had lived for generations. The train, travelling through the night, as it once took my grandfather from Chernivtsi to Lviv (or Lemberg, it would have been then) to Kraków and then Bremen or Hamburg, for his long journey to North America and another life. *Impossible now to think of train travel without a kind of tenderness.* I remember the sound of the whistle as we approached our final station, early morning, each village awake too in its place, lights extinguished for the day.

Exhibit 4 | bumpy road to Ivankivtsi

The roads are museum-worthy themselves, cobble easing to gravel, rubble, potholes so deep that a tire might never surface again. Vasyl drove carefully and well, talking, asking questions, taking a brief look at the photographs I'd packed in my suitcase. Cobblestone Freeway had arranged for him to drive us and to translate when we arrived.

Approaching the village, through poplars and fields, goldenrod, evergreen trees I thought must be silver fir, glimpses of water. Patches of gardens, some walled with stone, and fruit trees heavy with apples and pears.

> In the garden beside the water
> A tree is bending down.[5]

We stopped to ask a baba on the roadside if she knew of Kishkans in the village. She put down her pail of water with two apples floating on top and thought. No, she didn't think she did. But she pointed the way to the village building where the mayor was happy to talk to us. He couldn't think of any Kishkans but his assistant, who was on holiday, might know; she'd recently prepared a report on village history. He would call the priest, he said, picking up the phone, and ask him to meet us at the church. Two churches, because the old one still stands, and is still in use for special occasions. My grandfather was christened there in 1879, one Emanuel Nititovici performing the rites. It's an example of the house style, it doesn't have onion domes, it isn't a cruciform. The new one beside it is much more elaborate.

On our way to the church, we stopped at the war memorial commemorating those who died in the First World War. Can you see it, asked Vasyl, and yes, yes, I could: П. Кишкан. A family passed us in a wagon pulled by a horse. When we got out of the car again, my daughter stooped to play with three puppies by the store.

A man was waiting for us at the church. Not the priest, not yet, though he was on his way. This man was about John's age, early to mid-seventies, and no, he didn't know Kishkans. But he pointed to where the school once stood, before the bigger one was built, and he said he took French classes there though he could no longer remember any of it. He had a key and opened the old church first. It was filled with carpets, pictures, some of them clipped from magazines, and many many bouquets of artificial flowers, lengths of embroidered cloth, chairs stacked against the wall. We celebrate Mass here at Christmas, he said, and Easter. At least I think this is what he said. He and Vasyl were talking a mile a minute and every now and then Vasyl would turn to me to tell me what they were discussing. We went outside and there was the priest, striding through the grass by the new church.

He listened to Vasyl, nodding to me from time to time. No, he didn't know of any Kishkans but he would ask his wife, who spoke English. He spoke at length about the church. It was 250 years old, or maybe 300. (I read online that it was built in 1794 which made it 225 years old when I did the simple math. But probably the priest knows something that I don't, or maybe he's just awfully proud of it.) The old church was protected as a heritage building. I thanked the priest and the kind man who'd met us earlier. That man looked at me and said something. He is telling you that maybe he almost remembers the Kishkans, Vasyl said quietly. I held out my hand and the priest kissed it. Thank you, I told him, d'akuju, d'akuju. He smiled and waved us away.

There's an old cemetery, Vasyl told me, but it hasn't been kept up. The stones are pretty illegible. Do you want to try? And I decided no. I felt I'd found what I could. A name on a war memorial. The peace of a wooden church in sunlight, a wagon passing, a baba taking a bucket of water to an animal, another one leading a cow by a rope to the common pasture. Fields and gentle hills and trees on the horizon. The murmur of bees in the hollyhocks by the church gate. Buttercups, clover, silverweed, and nettles grew on the side of the road. I inhaled the scent of poplars and dust.

My husband and daughter touched my shoulders as I tucked myself into the car. In Ivankivtsi, we are almost remembered. We drove away and all I could think of was the long distance from

Chernivtsi to Lviv to Kraków to Bremen (or Hamburg), my grandfather walking with a small valise, his mother's bread and sausage wrapped in cloth, two photographs carefully tucked away, his shoes heavy with Ivankivtsi dust. Watch him. Watch him look back, take a deep breath of wood smoke and specific pollens that will settle in his lungs for the rest of his years. Almost remembered by the old church, a name carved in stone.

Exhibit 5 | lamps in Tulova cemetery

> Rivers a-plenty can be found here—
> But dry the bed now:
> And youths, brave, gallant youths, are countless,
> But they are dead now![6]

We were greeted by a group of villagers in traditional clothes. They sang to us. A woman stepped forward with warm bread wrapped in an embroidered cloth and we all broke pieces off the loaf. They took us into their church, shared by Orthodox worshippers and Catholics in what appeared to be a harmonious arrangement. We also walked through the cemetery and it was the first time I saw so many lamps on graves. I remember the Jewish cemetery in Kolín, in the Czech Republic, a place of broken stones and dense ivy growth and remnants of dozens of candles in puddled wax. And somehow (though I'm not a believer) the presence of God.

In Tulova, there were chickens on the little hill with the war memorial, women in a field with buckets, gathering potatoes. It was hot. Dusty. Thistles had gone to seed on the edge of the path. A man led a cow by a rope tied to one gnarly horn, clouds of dust rising from their feet, the one set cloven, the other rubber-booted. When we arrived at the place where our lunch was waiting, I needed to pee. The toilet was a hole in a wooden floor, a roll of paper hanging from the wall by a string. A tiny trickle of water in an old sink, a bar of rough soap, a coarse towel. The table was laid with platters of meat and cheese, bread, more than enough to make a meal of, but food kept arriving: bowls of borscht and dishes of smetana to add to it for extra flavour; varenyky filled with potato and soft cheese, crisp onions scattered over top, with more of that soured cream to dollop on your serving; banusz, or cornmeal, cooked in sour cream, flavoured with salo, and served with mushroom gravy; cabbage rolls; glasses of moonshine or wine or Pepsi or all of them, one chasing the other until you remembered that you had to pee in the hole in the wooden floor and had to keep some semblance of balance. Dancing and music for what seems like hours, the moonshine flowing and faces reddening in the heat.

Nearby, the Prut River made its own sweet music, starlight and moonshine and winged insects hovering. I had never seen lamps in graveyards and now dream of their light.

Exhibit 6 | a market in Kosiv, imagined again

Approaching the market, I passed an old woman entering the little roadside chapel, a sack of potatoes and a sack of onions leaning against it. A long row of babas with tiny tables. Jars of smetana, bowls of fresh cheese, big jars and water bottles filled with milk, topped with yellow cream, a cage of young ducks, baskets of squash, burlap sacks lumpy with apples. They held up bags of curds as I lingered by their tables.

Then the textiles: the long lengths of cross-stitch I'd seen draping every image in the Orthodox churches; blouses so beautiful I felt despair at where to begin (I bought one that day, another two days later); aprons, dresses embellished with roses and poppies; tables piled high with bolts of fabric you could buy by the metre (and I didn't. Which I now regret...); booths of liznyky, some elegant, some rough, and all of them smelling faintly of sheep. I paused by benches featuring tools and parts for chainsaws, homemade mouse and rat traps, garden rakes, used harnesses, mattocks, buckets; kiosks of ceramics; baskets of garlic, sacks of onions; wooden toys; three kittens in a box; antique Hutsul clothing, including boots, vests, jackets bright with embroidery.

Follow your nose to the booth laden with loaves of every shape and size. Doughnuts, nobbly buns, pastries filled with prunes or poppyseeds. Bottles of moonshine, carefully labelled, with tiny glasses for tasting. There were tables piled high with plastic plates, old brown pottery crocks, headscarves, and tiny thong underpants. Bows and arrows, slingshots, chickens hung by their feet. I bought two small oil paintings in wooden frames; they showed the same view of the valley I saw as I walked to the pool each morning. How much, I asked, and the artist, Mr. Пенета, carefully wrote 200 UAH on an old envelope. Ten dollars, more or less. Using a voice app on his phone, he told me that he was an artist and he lived in Kosiv. You're lucky, I replied. And I'm lucky too to have found your work.

On the bridge over the Rybnytsya River, a woman stopped me. She had four porcini mushrooms and a little jar of rosehips. I thought of my own jam made with *Rosa canina* hips, each one emptied of its coarse seeds, then boiled with sugar and lemon slices. No, I gestured, no, but what beautiful mushrooms! Pizza? And that was a word she knew. Her smile warmed me all the way back to the parking lot.

Digression

Everything I am remembering is burnished with moonshine, the taste of cherry-filled varenyky, sweet butter on dark bread. Mornings I swam in an unheated pool, the bottom littered with drowned insects, while all around me mist rose from the valley below our mountain slope. The mountains above me, source of the Dniester, Tisza, and Vistula Rivers, the upper streams of the Black Cheremosh and the White, the Prut. I thought of those mountains forming a long spine to the Beskydys in the Czech Republic, where my grandmother was born, two years after my grandfather, though they didn't meet until 1919, in the badlands of Alberta, she a widow, and him? I have no idea of his romantic history, though in his small archive of papers there are two photographs, one of two women, taken in Chernivtsi, one of whom resembles him enough to be a sister, and another of a woman with a generous mouth, dressed in a fur vest like the Hutsul women wore. Everything I am remembering, burnished with light too faint to read by, like the moonlight that came through my curtains at Sokilske, haunting the room like old history.

Exhibit 7 | above Tiudiv

At each farm, someone is picking apples, by ladder, by filling a bucket with windfalls. A man, a woman with a child, a couple with a basket between them. Stooks stand in the fields. Horses graze, dogs sleep as though dead in the dry grass. There are pumpkins still in the gardens, heaps of watermelons, horseradish leaves lush by the houses. At the farm where we turn to climb the road to Sokilske, an old table is balanced under a pear tree and a family is seated around it. The man raises his glass. A horse lifts its head as our wheels spin briefly, gaining traction for the steep rise. We can almost smell the Cheremosh River. And listen—there are chickadees in the sunflowers. Chickens scatter at the side of the road.

Open the doors to the namesakes who have driven from Ivankivtsi, bearing champagne, chocolates, a length of beautiful rushnyk, stitched in red with the symbol for a sown field, fertility, glowing with life. Sit at a table in the open lobby, all of you making marks on a paper: this one, and this one, and this one. They heard about you on Sunday in church, the priest's wife sharing news of your visit. And they've driven all that way on the rough roads to embrace you, to say their own names, the names of those who went to Canada. They have photographs and you show them the women your grandfather carried with him, the ones who ended up in the Moirs Happiness Package with an army book, a travel book giving him permission to leave but not to return.

At breakfast there is homemade butter for the bread, and uzvar, a juice made with dried apples and prunes. Over the valley below smoke hangs where someone is burning leaves, ghosts of trees and vines hovering until evening.

Exhibit 8 | in Yavoriv, the river is life

She leads you under maples to a room piled with blankets and carpets. On the way you'd asked the driver to stop so you could photograph fleeces drying after their preliminary washing in the Rybnytsya River. And here's what the fleeces become, grey, creamy white, charcoal, black, and a strange shade of henna. She shows you the steps to making a completed blanket. The wool is washed and dried, combed, then spun, a loom is warped with fine tight thread, and softer yarn is woven in and out of the warped threads. Once a piece is complete—a rug, a small cover for a stool or bench, or a big thick blanket—she takes it down a ladder to where a channel of the nearby Rybnytsya River has been directed through the valylo, big wooden tubs or tumbles; the textiles are battered by the force of the water, the threads tightening and shrinking, for three hours or eight, depending on the season and the temperature of the water. She pulls blankets from the water with a forked stick and says, The river is life.

Exhibit 9 | *in Bukovets, they are re-enacting a wedding*

We arrive to the wedding in a van holding twenty people. The villagers greet us with horilka made with golden root or mountain ginseng, sweet rolls, little toasts spread with salo. A wedding bower is set up on grass between two houses, with two long tables framing the area. Below us, the green lawn slopes away to the most beautiful valley, a cow here, soft trees there, a hut, the sound of geese and ducks in a pond below us. The bride's hair is braided with ribbons and coins, she is dressed in a smock intricately embroidered with poppies and roses, and aproned front and back, her waist bound with a long sash. Her groom is just as splendid. While her headdress is being arranged, women sing. More horilka is distributed to guests.

A few hours later we are eating a feast at the long tables. Platters of meat and cheese, cabbage salad, fresh bread, pale yellow butter, cucumbers flecked with dill, bowls of borscht, peppers stuffed with rice and onions, varenyky, bowls of rich smetana, dishes of pork in rich gravy over creamy potatoes, doughnuts light as air. Toast after toast to the couple (who are only pretending to be married so that we can witness the rituals), the guests whom we number ourselves among, the people of the village, young and old. We dance the old dances, whirling in the warm air, and laughing so hard that you can't tell who speaks Ukrainian, who doesn't. It all sounds like happiness.

When it was time to leave, our host, the young schoolteacher who lives in one of the houses framing the location, told us (partly in English, partly in animated Ukrainian translated by our guide) to remember that this was our land, that we must return, that we should bring our children, and our grandchildren. Your land, he emphasized. You are welcome here.

Exhibit 10 | everything rises from the Cheremosh River, a walled house, a steep path to the Church of the Nativity of the Virgin, a woman leading a skinny cow paused on the bridge

In the ancient wooden church in Kryvorivnya, the gospel is worn thin from kisses.

Exhibit 11 | *drawings and notes from William Kurelek's* To My Father's Village

I remember the pleasure of seeing William Kurelek's painting *Green Sunday* in the National Gallery in Ottawa. The painting commemorates Zeleni Sviata, the first Sunday in May when poplar branches would be placed in all four corners of a living room to welcome spring after a long hard winter. Kurelek's father came to Canada from Borivtsi, a village in Bukovina (or Bukovyna), in 1923. The painting felt like a kind of gift. After all, my own grandfather came to North America from Ivankivtsi, just seventeen kilometres from Borivtsi. He arrived on the Eastern Seaboard of the United States and eventually made his way to Drumheller where he met my grandmother and married her around 1920. Other Kishkans (or Kizkans or Kiszkans or Chişcanucs) had come to North America before him. And some came after. A cousin had immigrated to Saskatchewan (he was the father of the great Toronto Maple Leafs goalie John Bower, whose original surname was Kiszkan). I don't know how close family members were before they immigrated or the degree to which they kept in touch afterwards. My grandfather sent money to Bukovina to pay for the passage of another cousin. My father remembered that his father had been raised at least some of his childhood in the Sniatyn home of grandparents—my great-great-grandparents—with other cousins. I don't know if this was because the parents of the cousins were unable to care for them or because (perhaps) they needed help or could provide opportunities unavailable in Ivankivtsi. Sometimes I think these things will never be known and sometimes they appear to hover just beyond my consciousness, enticing me to work harder, dig deeper. (In this exhibit, the map will be faded, with blank areas. A hatchwork of trees, a long blue river.)

After seeing the Kurelek painting in November, I discovered that he'd gone to his father's village twice—for a four-hour visit in 1970 (the days of the old Soviet bureaucracy) and then just before his death in 1977. He kept notes and sketches of those trips, gathered together as a book: *To My Father's Village*.[7] His father had drawn maps for him and he found them surprisingly accurate. He found cousins, simple houses, many geese and ducks, and ancient pear trees. He drew the farm tools and kitchen implements, simple arrangements of sausages and bread spread with bacon fat, the fields and gardens, the sheaves tied for winter. He made beautiful paintings based on many of these things and it's clear that he intended to make more; he died just a few weeks after he returned from the second trip.

Reading Kurelek's letters home to his wife Jean in which he describes his father's village are in a way palimpsests. I hear a hidden history, my grandfather's, in his words. "Three-hundred-year-old pear trees such as my father used to hide in if caught stealing." "There was the pich and even the place on it where father said they used to sleep. The cheap calendar icons, the little windows, the loaf of bread on the bed, the pail of slops." (The pich was the traditional clay oven, with narrow shelves for bowls and beds.) This could almost be my grandparents' home in Beverly where we visited them as children. There was no pich in that house but there was bread, a bucket for scraps to scatter for the chickens, religious calendars on the kitchen walls.

(Maybe this is the way we discover our ancestors. They are short syllables in the stories of others—a stove, the brushes for whitewashing the walls of the two-roomed houses, a few ducks by the edge of a pond. I wish for more but am grateful to have at least this much. For this exhibit, make little stars where the villages should be. The road—rubbled areas, then some quite smooth. Expect grass, expect poplars and beeches, the odd chicken foraging in front of a house as you pass Yuzhynets' and Stavchany.)

There are hints in *To My Father's Village* of my own story. "Kurelek's father came to Canada following a visit to Borivtsi by a member of the Cunard Shipping Line." A few years ago I read a book about emigration from Bukovina that mentioned my grandfather's village specifically and detailed the numbers of men who left in a wave before the First World War. They didn't leave because they wanted to, necessarily. They were poor and hungry and they came for a better life. That improved life sometimes skipped a generation. Or two. I am the beneficiary of that sacrifice. Driving to Ivankivtsi, Vasyl detailed the route my grandfather probably took: Chernivtsi to Lviv to Kraków and then to Bremen or Hamburg where he would sail for Ellis Island, in steerage, as my grandmother from the other end of the Carpathian Mountains travelled to Canada. The cost for the trip to North America? Ninety to 120 US dollars. I thought of them both as I curled up in the crisp sheets on the train from Kyiv to Chernivtsi, my own relative luxury unimaginable to them.

On Kurelek's last visit to Borivtsi, he went to the fields to paint and a child found him with his face in the dirt. "I'm alright," Kurelek assured him. "I'm only searching for my roots."

> My dear mother, what will happen to me if I die in a
>   foreign land?
> Well, my dearest, you will be buried by other people.[8]

Under the earth, tubers and roots, ancient trees spreading wide their branches. For this exhibit, open the book to the drawing of a fork deep within a hill of potatoes. One potato is impaled on a tine. Collect them in buckets, in burlap sacks. Come, sit. Rest. Every person who has lived in these villages is welcome to share the green shade. (This is your land too, said the schoolteacher at Bukovets. You are welcome.)

Exhibit 12 | *the villages and block settlements of Alberta*

Star, Shandro, Bolan, Toporvitsi, North Kotzman, Buchach, Podola, Luzan, Smoky Lake, Myrnam, Musidora, South River. I don't believe my grandfather knew these places. They were not what he came to. What did he come to? What did he come for? I look at photographs of the buildings—the grain elevator from a village now dissolved; a burdei, or dugout structure, where a family might have lived for years until a true house could be built, a clay-plastered log home, saddle-notched, a four-sided hip-gabled roof, thatched with straw or marsh grass; the churches with their elegant domes; a schoolhouse; barns collapsing into earth. I look at the men on flimsy pole scaffolding building a church in Alberta and try to imagine my grandfather among them. I know he was in Phoenix, BC, in 1911. I know (or hearsay has it) that he was working in a mine at Kananaskis—Ribbon Creek or maybe Ings Mine?—when the First World War broke out and he was told to leave, no pay issued, so he walked home. But where was home then? The sturdy communities of farmers were not his. I can't find him in Zhoda, Borshchiw, New Kiew, South Kotzman, and Pazan.

Exhibit 13 | *an empty case*

I didn't go to Valyava or the Museum of the Multitude Village. The opportunity never presented itself and I now know that the roads were rough, the signposts almost invisible. When Vasyl drove us to Ivankivtsi, he stopped three times to ask people the way. Their hands would drift in the air like falling leaves—it was mid-September and some of the leaves were turning, turning, lingering in the air as they left the tree—but Vasyl knew the signals. A narrow turn between the trees? Past the field where you could see a lake? I imagined asking a baba on the side of the road, Where is the Museum of the Multitude Village, and her looking away, touching her cow's neck with a stick. Move on, move on.

The namesakes (my name and my great-grandmother's maiden name) who visited—call them cousins, distant sisters. The patriarch with his gold tooth and wild eyebrows who resembled your grand-father? Call him your deda once removed—they knew the village and one of them said, when I mentioned Vasily Kishkan, "He wrote a book." (I've tried to find out what kind of book but haven't had any luck.) The photographs of the museum in Valyava show a room featuring a stove with a shelf for children to sleep on, a mannequin at a spinning wheel, a trunk. Did my great-grandmother spin wool? Did my grandfather pack his worldly possessions in the family trunk to take with him to Bremen or Hamburg and then to Franklin Furnace, New Jersey, his destination?

I have no idea of his romantic history, though in his small archive of papers there are two photographs, one of two women, taken in Chernivtsi (this is printed on the back), one of whom resembles him enough to be a sister, and another of a single woman with a generous mouth, dressed in a fur vest like the Hutsul women wore, and wear still in Bukovets on a high hill overlooking the valley while the wedding dancers whirl in sunlight. He kept the photographs all his life.

The wild wind bloweth ever,
The tree's high branches shaking.

His letter cometh never—
And ah, my heart is breaking![9]

In the dust, my grandfather's footsteps, not worth displaying. His name—our name—on an old monument. The baba put down her pail of water with two apples floating on top, and thought. She was not the oldest woman in the village but old enough to have her ear to the ground, on the line of names that might be spoken at church, in the store selling bread, pumpkins, canisters of fuel, names running like the roots of spreading trees. No, it wasn't a name she knew, though several of the distant relations who came bearing gifts also bear my (our) name. I sense a mystery. Perhaps there's a story there, a village vendetta, a divide uncrossed. Yet before I knew of those relations, before they came to Sokilske with champagne and rushnyk and photographs, someone almost remembered, the man who opened the church and showed me the windows, squares of red and blue glass filtering daylight so beautifully that I see the interior as anyone ever here saw it. I am my great-grandmother walking home from Mass, filled with sorrow at the loss of a son heading to the train. The cow needs to be taken to the commonage, a rope tied to her horn, led to the fields of long grass and poplars starting to turn gold. There is nothing to display in this case, no intricate diorama of a house with green shutters, surrounded by sunflowers, no wagon, the card with our name blank, edges curled a little with age.

Acknowledgements

I AM GRATEFUL to my family and friends who encourage and provide inspiration on a daily basis. I am also grateful to the BC Arts Council for financial support (out of the blue).

"Love Song" is for my children, their partners, their children, and my husband (lyrics reprinted with permission).

> No matter how long it takes
> You can't hurry love
> No, you just have to wait

"The River Door" is for my cousin, Amanda Reiter.

"Museum of the Multitude Village" was written after an exhilarating visit to Ukraine and the village my paternal grandfather left in 1907. My husband John Pass and my daughter Angelica Pass accompanied me to Ivankivtsi, and beyond, and I loved their company. This essay is for them. (Budmo!)

"We are still here" was written for the anthology, *Locations of Grief: An Emotional Geography*, edited by Catherine Owen (Wolsak & Wynn, 2020). "A Dark Path" appeared in *Brick* 104. An abbreviated version of

"How Rivers Break Away and Meet Again" was published in *The Clearing*, the online journal of Little Toller Books (https://www. littletoller.co.uk/the-clearing/essay/how-rivers-break-away-and-meet-again-by-theresa-kishkan/). "Love Song" was written for the anthology *The Summer Book*, edited by Mona Fertig (Mother Tongue Publishing, 2017). I am grateful to the editors who helped me refine the essays they chose to publish. "Museum of the Multitude Village" was printed as a gift to my friends and family to celebrate my sixty-fifth birthday. I thank my husband for printing cover label, title page, and colophon on our 19th century Chandler and Price platen press and my dear friend Anik See for layout of the text.

Librarians and archivists have been so generous. I'd like to thank Peter Peller at the University of Calgary for his help in locating maps and my son Forrest Pass at Library and Archives Canada for providing considerable assistance in accessing materials I never dreamed existed.

Two anonymous readers gave me detailed suggestions to make this a better book. Thank you. The entire team at University of Alberta Press has been helpful and enthusiastic: a gift. And to Kimmy Beach, who provided editorial expertise as well as exuberant guidance, my heartfelt gratitude.

Notes

Preface

1. John D'Agata, "John D'Agata Redefines the Essay," interview by Susan Steinberg, *Electric Literature*, July 14, 2016, https://electricliterature.com/john-dagata-redefines-the-essay/.

A Dark Path

1. This and subsequent passages from *The Inferno of Dante* are translated by Robert Pinsky.
2. Bernardo's "Who's there?" and Francisco's further "Nay, answer me. Stand and unfold yourself" are the opening lines of *Hamlet*.

The Blue Etymologies

1. I spent ages looking at various dictionary definitions—etymonline.com is fascinating but a bit of a rabbit hole—and I realized that sometimes less is more. This is the first entry in my university (mid-1970s) edition of *The Concise Oxford Dictionary of Current English*, fifth edition.
2. *Shorter Oxford English Dictionary on Historical Principles,* sixth edition, volume 1, A – M (a perfect companion, rested on one's lap, to morning coffee by the fire).
3. Wada, *Memory*, 8. This is a revelatory book about surface design in general and the far-reaching possibilities of shibori in particular. After reading it, my relationship to fabric and the process of dyeing it shifted slightly, felt more sculptural.
4. A woman buried sometime between 1000 and 1200 AD in a small monastery for women in Dalheim, Germany, was found to have lapis lazuli in the calculus on her lower jaw, almost certainly from her work, over many years, as a scribe using ultramarine, a costly pigment made from lapis lazuli. Only experienced scribes

would have access to such an expensive pigment, used along with gold leaf and silver to embellish religious texts.

5.   *Shorter Oxford English Dictionary*.

6.   This charming book was used by artists and naturalists in the nineteenth century, including Charles Darwin, who took a copy with him on the H M S *Beagle* (1831–1836) and used Werner's nomenclature to record his notes on zoology. Patrick Syme, who studied with a student of Abraham Werner, added to Werner's key to identifying minerals by key characteristics, including colour, using the taxonomy for other members of the animal, vegetable, and mineral kingdoms.

7.   The passages of Derek Jarman are from his last book, *Chroma*, 91.

8.   Oliver Sacks, from his essay "Altered States," 110.

9.   The story of the discovery of the Chauvet Cave in 1994 and its extraordinary galleries of art has been told in many places. A good place to begin is with one of several books written by Jean Clottes, former director of prehistoric antiquities for the Midi-Pyrénées region of France.

10.   This passage from fifteenth-century scholar-priest Marsilio Ficino's *Three Books on Life* appears in Jarman's *Chroma*, 91.

11.   This passage is from David Lewis-Williams's study of paleolithic cave art, in which he advances the theory that the art was created in shamanic rituals in part facilitated by the use of psychotropic substances. *The Mind in the Cave*, 121.

We Are Still Here

1.   This essay adopts the form of movements from Bach's Violin Partita No. 2 in D Minor, B W V 1004, and takes up Christopher Hogwood's challenge to learn to dance (through grief and loss), quoted in Clark's article "Deconstructing the Genius of Bach," in *Limelight*.

2.   Shakespeare, "Sonnet 3," line 9, 1453.

3.   John Berger, from his story "Le Pont d'Arc," 136.

4.   Johann Mattheson, a Baroque musician and music theorist, writing about Bach.

5.   Woolf, "A Dance at Queen's Gate," 165.

6.   Brahms and Schumann, *Letters*, 16.

Blue Portugal

1.   The passages of verse threaded through this essay are from Leoš Janáček's *Moravian Folk Poetry in Song*, based on the folk poetry of his birthplace, Hukvaldy, in what is now the Czech Republic.

2.   I did tumble down the rabbit hole of the probable origins of the *Vitis vinifera* variety known as Modrý Portugal in the Czech Republic where I first tasted it. This passage is taken from an article published by the Institute for Grapevine Breeding in Germany, devoted to the origins of the grape known as Modrý Portugal, Portugais Bleu, Blauer Portugieser, and Kékoportó, among other names, depending on place of cultivation. Maul et al., "The 'Missing Link,'" 138.

3.   Maul et al., "The 'Missing Link,'" 138.

4.   I read several reports on steerage conditions and one, the "US Immigration Report on Steerage—1911" from the Gjenvick-Gjønvik Archives website, gave me insight into the voyage as my grandmother might have experienced it. https://www.gjenvick.com/Immigration/Steerage/USImmigrationReportOnSteerageConditions-1911.html.

5.   Sometimes a phrase enters your thinking. "Geographical loneliness," noted at an exhibition in Belem, near Lisbon, in 2015, is one of those phrases. I thought of my grandmother, lonely for her own home as she travelled to Canada and made a new life for herself in a landscape very different from the one she left; and I also experience that loneliness myself, bereft of the landscapes where I lived as a child and knew her. Martins et al., *O Tempo*, 126.

6.   I don't speak Czech and relied on an article in Czech, painstakingly translated one word at a time using online dictionaries, to figure out the etymology of the Lomná River, a tributary of the Olza, running by my grandmother's house in Horni Lomná. DBpedia, "Lomná (river)," https://dbpedia.org/page/Lomn%C3%A1_(river).

7.   This passage by Leoš Janáček's, comes from a paper, "The Musical Realism of Leoš Janáček," written by Tiina Vainiomäki, a Finnish musicologist (p. 328). She cites as its source, "The System of Sciences for Music Recognition," an article by Janáček, published between 1919 and 1921, though I haven't been able to track it down.

8.   Maul et al., "The 'Missing Link,'" 142.

9.   The young pianist is Zoltán Fejérvári. I was lucky enough to hear him play a beautiful programme of Robert Schumann, Béla Bartók, and Leoš Janáček in 2019.

10.   Until her death in 2018, in her nineties, Anežka Kašpárková painted the windows and doors of her Czech village, Louka, with traditional Moravian floral designs in vivid blue.

11.   In a letter written in 1908, Leoš Janáček commented on the individual pieces in his piano cycle, *On an Overgrown Path*. The second of these pieces, "A Leaf Blown by the Wind," was "a love-song."

12.   The wine is described this way on the website for the Baloun Winery ("Vinařstzí Baloun"), www.baloun.cz.

How Rivers Break Away and Meet Again

1.   From Virginia Woolf's essay "A Sketch of the Past," 98.

2.   From the poem "Alone, Looking for Blossoms Along the River," by Tu Fu, or Du Fu, in David Hinton's translation. *Selected Poems*, 60.

3.   *Wikipedia*, "Fraser Pass," https://en.wikipedia.org/wiki/Fraser_Pass.

4.   This comes from the 1848 section of David Thompson's writing on his travels. Thompson, 196.

5.   This is a passage from "[50] L. to the Nymphs [Nymphai]," one of the pre-classical poems known as the Orphic Hymns, composed not by Orpheus but rather by a

number of unknown poets associated with his cult. *Theoi Texts Library*, https://www.theoi.com/Text/OrphicHymns2.html#50.

6. Passages of the Song of Songs from the Old Testament are threaded through this section (E S V, Song: 1:1, 1:17, 2:7). https://www.esv.org/.

7. The epigraph to this section is from the opening of Bruce Hutchison's contribution to *The Rivers of America Series* (it's #42 in the series). I've known this river all my life, from early years in Matsqui, on its banks, to walks along its estuary to explorations up its canyons and tributaries, have seen it in high water season, and low, and agree that it is (or can be) "...mad, ravenous and lonely." Hutchinson, 5.

8. This passage comes from *The Letters and Journals of Simon Fraser, 1806–1808*, 103.

9. Fraser, *Letters*, 129.

10. Fraser, *Letters*, 108.

11. Fraser, *Letters*, 100.

12. One of the single most beautiful sentences I've ever read, the conclusion of Norman Maclean's novella *A River Runs Through It*, 161.

Blueprints

1. *Lexico*, "blueprint," https://www.lexico.com/en/definition/blueprint.

2. There are a number of websites devoted to the cyanotypes of Anna Atkins. This one is a good place to start: New York Public Library, "Blue Prints: The Pioneering Photographs of Anna Atkins," https://www.nypl.org/events/exhibitions/blue-prints-pioneering-photographs-anna-atkins.

3. I wanted to know how much I was remembering correctly and also I wanted to refresh my sense of the process of translating anticipated space (rooms, decks, stairwells) to paper, then to an actual structure. I asked my husband John Pass these questions.

Love Song

1. From "You Can't Hurry Love," recorded in 1966 by The Supremes. Words and Music by Edward Holland Jr., Lamont Dozier and Brian Holland. Copyright © 1965 Stone Agate Music. Copyright Renewed. All Rights Administered by Sony Music Publishing L L C, 424 Church Street, Suite 1200, Nashville, TN 37219. International. Copyright Secured All Rights Reserved. *Reprinted by Permission of Hal Leonard L L C*.

The River Door

1. This is cited in the translator's introduction to Ines Cagnati's novel, *Free Day*, viii.

2. Provincial Archives of Alberta, Alberta Homestead Records, Accession 1970.313, Film 2539, File 31177 (hereafter A H R), 169.

3. I entered Joseph Yopek's surname into the search function of the Homestead Index of the Alberta Genealogical Society: https://www.abgenealogy.ca/ab-homestead-index-page.

4. *The Hills of Home*, a history of the Drumheller Valley, has many personal histories of pioneer families in the valley as well as background history relating the development of the town and environs. Drumheller Valley History Association, 125.

5. Gertrude Charters was a member of a Volunteer Aid Detachment who had worked as a nursing aid in a Calgary hospital. She was recruited in early October 1918, to come to Drumheller to assist in caring for victims of the emerging Spanish flu epidemic. She remembered this period in "The 'Black Death' at Drumheller," *Maclean's*, March 5, 1966, 21.

6. *The Drumheller Mail* was an invaluable source of reporting, archival and contemporary. This comes from *The Drumheller Mail*, March 24, 2011. "Spanish Flu Paralyzes Early Drumheller," https://www.drumhellermail.com/featured/9667-spanish-flu-paralyzes-early-drumheller.

7. I puzzled over the absence of the names of my grandmother's first husband and her brother on documents listing successful purchasers of land at auction in 1917 and by luck found the listing for the auction in the *Hanna Herald* (September 20, 1917) with the proviso that certain people were ineligible to acquire lots.

8. The story of Mrs. Cattini appears in *The Hills of Home*, 147.

9. Mrs. Bond's story in *The Hills of Home* provided a window (of wavy glass) into my grandmother's life. *The Hills of Home*, 127.

10. Another story from *The Hills of Home*, 467.

11. *Concise Oxford Dictionary of Current English*, fifth edition.

12. *The Drumheller Mail*, October 4, 1918, 4.

13. *The Drumheller Mail*, October 31, 1918, 1.

14. Ibid., 8.

15. *Hanna Herald*, September 20, 1917.

16. *The Hills of Home*, 125.

17. Gertrude Charters, in *Maclean's*, 21.

18. I read about efforts to attract Ukrainian men to Canada in Vadim Kukushkin's *From Peasants to Labourers: Ukrainian and Belarusan Immigration from the Russian Empire to Canada* and was surprised to find mention of my grandfather's tiny village in Bukovina. Kukushkin, 34.

19. I don't know if Joseph Yopek, my grandmother's first husband, or her second husband, my grandfather John Kishkan, were active in the labour movement but reading this article from *Briarpatch* magazine has me hoping that they were. Kate Jacobson, April 30, 2018. https://briarpatchmagazine.com/articles/view/remembering-the-1919-drumheller-strike.

20. The common sense in this *Science* magazine article of May 30, 1919, echoes what we are being told in the current COVID-19 pandemic. George A. Soper, "The Lessons of the Pandemic." https://www.science.org/doi/10.1126/science.49.1274.501.

21. More advice from *Science* magazine, May 30, 1919. Soper, "The Lessons of the Pandemic."

22. This warning from an auction notice in the *Hanna Herald*, September 20, 1917, kept echoing as I searched for what happened to my grandmother and her family.

23. The formidable Gertrude Charters again. *Maclean's*, 27.

24. Ibid., 29.

25. *The Drumheller Mail*, October 31, 1918, 4.

26. A H R, Letter from Frank Collins, Department of the Interior, Office of the Superintendent of School Lands, Winnipeg, to Frank Checkley, Controller of School Lands, Department of the Interior, Ottawa, December 1, 1916.

27. A H R, Letter from Frank Collins to Frank Checkley.

28. A H R, Letter from Frank Checkley to Frank Collins.

29. A H R, Memorandum from E. Deville, Surveyor General, Department of the Interior, Topographical Survey Branch, to Controller of School Lands, Department of the Interior, Ottawa, April 11, 1917.

30. The Starland County Fonds are held at the Provincial Archives of Alberta in Edmonton. A complete description of the fonds can be accessed at https://hermis. alberta.ca/paa/Search.aspx?st=%22Starland+County+Fonds%22.

Museum of the Multitude Village

1. Pamuk, *The Museum*, 520.

2. From the English version of the website *IGotoWorld.com*: https://ua.igotoworld. com/en/poi_object/69387_muzey-istorii-sela-valyava.htm.

3. This (from "In the Fields Grows the Rye"), and all subsequent lines of verse, are from *Songs of Ukraina*, translated by Florence Randal Livesay.

4. *Railtracks* is a correspondence, a dialogue between John Berger and Anne Michaels, taking place against a backdrop of Tereza Stehlíková's moody photographs of Bohemia. Berger and Michaels, 69.

5. Livesay, from "In the Garden Beside the Water."

6. Livesay, from "The Kalina" (old folk song).

7. All quotations from Kurelek come from *To My Father's Village*, published in 1988.

8. From "Plyve Kacha Po Tysini." See "An Old Ukranian Folk Song Takes on New Meaning in the Current Crisis," https://theworld.org/stories/2014-04-16/ old-Ukrainian-folk-song-takes-new-meaning-current-crisis.

9. Livesay, from "The Two Lovers" (fragment).

Sources

Books

Alighieri, Dante. *The Inferno of Dante*. Translated by Robert Pinsky. New York: Farrar, Straus and Giroux, 1994.

Berger, John. "Le Pont d'Arc." In *Here is Where We Meet*. New York: Random House, 2005.

Berger, John, and Anne Michaels, with photographs by Tereza Stehlíková. *Railtracks*. Berkeley, CA: Counterpoint Press, 2013.

Brahms, Johannes, and Clara Schumann. *Letters of Clara Schumann and Johannes Brahms, 1853–1896*. Edited by Berthold Litzmann. 2 vols. Westport, CT: Hyperion Press, 1979.

Cagnati, Ines. *Free Day*. Translated by Liesl Schillinger. New York: N Y R B Classics, 2019.

Canadian Social Studies Atlas, re-issue. Toronto and Vancouver: J.M. Dent & Sons, 1952.

Clottes, Jean. *Chauvet Cave: The Art of Earliest Times*. Translated by Paul Bahn. Salt Lake City: University of Utah Press, 2003.

Concise Oxford Dictionary of Current English, fifth edition. London: Oxford University Press, 1964.

D'Agata, John. *The Lost Origins of the Essay*. Minneapolis, MN: Greywolf Press, 2009.

———. *The Making of the American Essay*. Minneapolis, MN: Greywolf Press, 2016.

Drumheller Valley History Association. *The Hills of Home: Drumheller Valley*. Drumheller, AB: Drumheller Valley History Association, 1973.

Fraser, Simon. *The Letters and Journals of Simon Fraser, 1806–1808*. Edited by W. Kaye Lamb. Toronto: Dundurn Press, 2007.

A Greek–English Lexicon, ninth edition. Oxford: Clarendon Press, 1999.

Hutchison, Bruce. *The Fraser*. New York: Rinehart and Company, 1950.

Janáček, Leoš, Leoš Faltus, Svatava Přibáňová, and Eva Drlíková. *Theoretical Works: Articles, Studies, Lectures, Concepts, Fractures, Sketches, Testimonies (1877–1927)*. Brno: Editio Janáček, 2007.

Jarman, Derek. *Chroma: A Book of Colour*. New York: Vintage Publishing, 1995.

Kroetsch, Robert. *Badlands*. Toronto: New Press, 1975.

Kukushkin, Vadim. *From Peasants to Labourers: Ukrainian and Belarusan Immigration from the Russian Empire to Canada*. Montreal and Kingston: McGill-Queen's University Press, 2007.

Kurelek, William. *To My Father's Village*. Montreal: Tundra Books, 1988.

Lewis-Williams, David. *The Mind in the Cave: Consciousness and the Origins of Art*. London: Thames and Hudson, 2004.

Livesay, Florence Randal, trans., *Songs of Ukraina*. London: J.M. Dent & Sons, 1916.

Maclean, Norman. *A River Runs Through It*. Chicago: University of Chicago Press, 1976.

Martins, Adolfo Miguel, et al. *O Tempo Resgatado Ao Mar (Time Salvaged from the Sea)*. Translated by Carla Ventura, Maria João Nunes, Maria Empis, and John Porter. Lisbon: Museu Nacional de Arqueologia, 2014.

Mattheson, Johann. *Der vollkommene Capellmeister (The Perfect Chapelmaster)*. Translated by Ernest Harriss. Ann Arbor, MI: UMI Research Press, 1981.

McGovern, Patrick. *Ancient Wine: The Search for the Origins of Viniculture*. Princeton: Princeton University Press, 2003.

New Concise World Atlas, third edition. New York: Oxford University Press, 2009.

Pamuk, Orhan. *The Museum of Innocence*. Translated by Maureen Freely. Toronto: Vintage Canada, 2008.

Pocket Oxford Greek Dictionary, fifth edition. New York: Oxford University Press, 2000.

Sacks, Oliver. "Altered States." In *Hallucinations*. Toronto: Knopf Canada, 2012.

Shakespeare, William. "Antony and Cleopatra." In *The Complete Pelican Shakespeare, 1169–1211*, edited by Maynard Mack. Toronto: Penguin, 1977.

———. *Hamlet*. Edited by Sylvan Barnet. Toronto: Signet Classics, 1998.

———. "Sonnet 3." In *The Complete Pelican Shakespeare*. Toronto: Penguin, 1977.

Steinhardt, Arnold. *Violin Dreams*. Boston: Houghton Mifflin Harcourt, 2008.

Syme, Patrick. *Werner's Nomenclature of Colours: Adapted to Zoology, Botany, Chemistry, Mineralogy, Anatomy, and the Arts*. London: Natural History Museum, 2018.

Thompson, David. *The Writings of David Thompson, Volume 2: The Travels, 1848 Version, and Associated Texts*. Edited by William E. Moreau. Montreal and Kingston: McGill-Queen's University Press, 2015.

Tausky, Vilem and Margaret, ed. and trans. *Janáček: Leaves from His Life*. London: Kahn & Averill, 1982.

Tu Fu. *The Selected Poems of Tu Fu*. Translated by David Hinton. New York: New Directions Publishing, 1989.

Wada, Yoshiko Wamoto. *Memory on Cloth: Shibori Now*. New York: Kodansha USA, 2012.

Woolf, Virginia. "A Dance at Queen's Gate." In *A Passionate Apprentice: The Early Journals, 1897–1909*, edited by Mitchell A. Leaska. Boston: Houghton Mifflin Harcourt, 1992.

———. "A Sketch of the Past." In *Moments of Being: Unpublished Autobiographical Writings*, edited by Jeanne Schulkind. New York: Harcourt, Brace, Jovanovich, 1976.

Articles

Charters, Gertrude. "The 'Black Death' at Drumheller." *Maclean's*, March 5, 1966.

Clark, Philip. "Deconstructing the Genius of Bach." *Limelight*, September 6, 2013. https://www.limelightmagazine.com.au/features/deconstructing-the-genius-of-bach/.

D'Agata, John. "John D'Agata Redefines the Essay." Interview by Susan Steinberg. *Electric Literature*, July 14, 2016. https://electricliterature.com/john-dagata-redefines-the-essay/.

Jacobson, Kate. "Remembering the 1919 Drumheller Strike." *Briarpatch*, April 30, 2018. https://briarpatchmagazine.com/articles/view/remembering-the-1919-drumheller-strike.

Maul, E., F. Rockel, and R. Topfer. "The 'Missing Link' 'Blaue Zimmettraube' Reveals that 'Blauer Portugieser' and 'Blaufrankisch' Originated in Lower Styria." *Vitis: Journal of Grapevine Research* 55, no.3 (2016): 135–143.

Radini, A., et al. "Medieval Women's Early Involvement in Manuscript Production Suggested by Lapis Lazuli Identification in Dental Calculus." *Science Advances* 5, no. 1 (2019). https://advances.sciencemag.org/content/5/1/eaau7126.

Soper, George A. "The Lessons of the Pandemic." *Science* 49, no. 1274 (May 30, 1919): 501–506. https://www.science.org/doi/10.1126/science.49.1274.501.

"Spanish Flu Paralyzes Early Drumheller." *The Drumheller Mail*, March 24, 2011. https://www.drumhellermail.com/featured/9667-spanish-flu-paralyzes-early-drumheller.

"US Immigration Report on Steerage—1911." Gjenvick-Gjønvik Archives. https://www.gjenvick.com/Immigration/Steerage/USImmigrationReportOnSteerageConditions-1911.html.

Vainiomäki, Tiina. "The Musical Realism of Leoš Janáček." Doctoral dissertation, University of Helsinki, 2012. https://helda.helsinki.fi/bitstream/handle/10138/36087/themusic.pdf.

Discography

Hahn, Hilary. *Hilary Hahn Plays Bach*. Sony Classical Records, 1997.

Janková, Martina, Tomáš Král, and Ivo Kahánek. *Janáček: Moravian Folk Poetry in Song*. Supraphon, 2015.

Kvapil, Radoslav. *Janáček Piano Music: On an Overgrown Path, In the Mists, Piano Sonata*. Alto, 1994.

Perlman, Itzhak. *J.S. Bach: Complete Sonatas and Partitas*. Warner Classics, 2015.

Ross, Diana, and the Supremes. *The Best of Diana Ross and the Supremes: The Millennium Collection*. Universal Music Canada, 1999.

Other Titles from University of Alberta Press

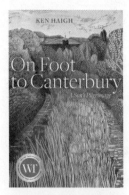

On Foot to Canterbury
A Son's Pilgrimage
KEN HAIGH

Ken Haigh explores the historical and literary landscape of the Pilgrims' Way in southern England.
Wayfarer Series

Tiny Lights for Travellers
NAOMI K. LEWIS

Vulnerable and funny, this award-winning memoir explores Jewish identity, family, the Holocaust, and belonging.
Wayfarer Series

Magnetic North
Sea Voyage to Svalbard
JENNA BUTLER

A sea voyage connecting continents traces the impacts of climate change on northern lands.
Wayfarer Series

More information at uap.ualberta.ca